The … for

the Last Day Church

MW01681401

by

Scott C. Lovett

Fervent Fire Productions

Tulsa, Oklahoma

Unless otherwise indicated, all Old and New Testament Scripture quotations are taken from the *King James Version, 1769 edition* of the Bible.

Scripture quotations marked "NLT" are taken from *Holy Bible, New Living Translation, Copyright 1996* by Tyndale Charitable Trust. All rights reserved.

The Great Search for the Last Day Church

ISBN 978-0-578-03937-4

Copyright © 2009 by Scott C. Lovett

Fervent Fire Evangelistic Ministries

315 S. Sheridan Road

Tulsa, Oklahoma 74112

Published by Fervent Fire Productions

315 S. Sheridan Road

Tulsa, Oklahoma 74112

Printed in the United States of America. All rights reserved under International Copyright Law. Contents and / or cover may not be reproduced in whole or in part in any form without the express written consent of the Publisher.

Dedication

I would like to dedicate *The Great Search for the Last Day Church* to my God, my Lord, my Savior, Jesus Christ, Who is looking for a people who are committed to, and in love with Him. To every leader and laborer of the Gospel who continue to submit themselves to the Holy Spirit and the infallible Word in order to prepare a body for our soon coming King. To the faithful saints who have reached their destination and patiently wait for the fulfillment of the declared promises of God to manifest in the earth. To the Godly influences in my life, who yielded to the Holy Spirit and spoke the truth so that I might have a relationship with the indwelling Word. To the members of my family who heard the truth and allowed Jesus Christ to change them so that the promise would remain secure to later generations. To my wife who stands in faith, endures in times of struggle, and remains in agreement with the work of God to the very end. To my children and heirs who by faithfulness will continue to receive the promise. To my local church family consisting of elders, deacons, and members who assist me in perfecting my calling through love and correction making my election sure. To our ministry partners who continue to see the vision and are faithful in support. To the people God has called me to minister to throughout America and around the world.

Contents

The Winds of Doctrine

For the eyes of the LORD run to and fro throughout the whole earth, to show himself strong in the behalf of them whose heart is perfect toward him.

2 Chronicles 16:9

With a grieving heart and searching eyes, the Lord is looking for His people. His eyes are searching and looking upon the hearts of men to find those who have a true inward desire to believe His Word and seek His truth. His everlasting love continues to seek out those who will love Him in return. In this hour it seems that congregations and denominations have forgotten that the eyes of the Lord see through the works of religion and man-made doctrine to the purpose and the true desire that lives in the heart.

As He searches, He finds many who are using His Word to bring about the fulfillment of personal lust. Within the world of the church, there are those who use religion to manipulate and control men to build earthly kingdoms that make men subservient to a creed, instead of causing them to yield to the Lord. Those who carry the true heart of God will always yield their beliefs to His Word so that their faith will not lie in the ideals and traditions of men.

In our day, the area of doctrine has become an issue that brings great division and pain within the body of Jesus Christ. Instead of men yielding to the Word, we have used the Word as a tool to bring division, rather than the unity that Jesus prayed for when He said,

"And the glory which thou gavest me I have given them; that they may be one, even as we are one: I in them, and thou in me, that they may be made perfect in one; and that the world may know that thou hast sent me, and hast loved them, as thou hast loved me." (John 17:22)

The intent of God is to bring a group of pure hearted people together who desire to believe His Word as it was intended from its originator, who is Jesus Himself. If this is God's purpose, then the church world is off course in building separate kingdoms, denominations, and doctrines. While the spirit of division reigns in the religious courts of men, in God's court there is no division. His eyes see the truth and in the end He knows them that are His.

God has never been and never will be deceived by denomination, false doctrine, or the congregational members who say they love Him, but fail to have a true heart towards His Word. He knows those who have used His Word to manipulate men and taught them to serve a doctrine or tradition instead of serving Him. Those who have true hearts after God want to know the truth. They will diligently seek the Lord in order to hear His voice and will follow His commands without compromise. They will let Jesus take them from glory to glory until they grow and reach a place of being as He is. Instead of arguing about what they believe, they will believe what His Word says. People after His heart will search until they find the truth that He longs to reveal. In Proverbs it says,

The tongue of the wise useth knowledge aright: but the mouth of fools poureth out foolishness. The eyes of the LORD are in every place, beholding the evil and the good. A wholesome tongue is a tree of life: but perverseness therein is a breach in the spirit. A fool despiseth his father's instruction: but he that regardeth reproof is prudent. In the house of the righteous is much treasure: but in the revenues of the wicked is trouble. The lips of the wise disperse knowledge: but the heart of the foolish doeth not so. (Proverbs 15:2-7)

As the eyes of the Lord are looking through the churches, He is not only judging the teachings being taught, and the doctrines being upheld, but is looking into the hearts of the leaders to see if the Word of God is being used in the right manner and intent. There is a right way and a wrong way to use the knowledge found within the pages of God's Word. If our intent is to teach people to find the Lord, then encourage them to go to the Word and seek out the truth that lies within its pages. The problem with the majority of denominations, churches, and leaders is that most of the time doctrine is used as a way to control the individual. We ask the individuals within our congregations to believe us based on our studies instead of encouraging them to search on their own to find Scripture that may oppose the doctrine we uphold. The majority of man-made kingdoms ask individuals who question their teachings to leave instead of taking another sincere look into the teachings they hold. Every breach within the Church is caused out of man's desire to be right instead of out of a sincere desire to follow Jesus. The Word is never wrong, it is always right. You notice that in the house of the righteous there is much treasure. This treasure is the revealed truth of God Himself. The wicked are limited to being motivated by revenues. Because the eyes of the Lord see through to the intent of the hearts, many denominations, churches, and ministries will be destroyed. Amos 9:8 says,

Behold, the eyes of the Lord GOD upon the sinful kingdom, and I will destroy it from off the face of the earth; saving that I will not utterly destroy the house of Jacob, saith the LORD.

God is looking into the hearts of every denomination and church group to see the intent that is held within. His eyes are reviewing our teachings and our doctrines to see if they are truly from Him. If we fail to find that place of being yielded we will be destroyed. The true church of Jesus Christ will be made one, whether by men becoming broken in denominational opinion, or by God becoming judge. As we approach the return of Jesus Christ, every one of us will be judged by what we believe. Proverbs 22:10-12 says,

Cast out the scorner, and contention shall go out; yea, strife and reproach shall cease. He that loveth pureness of heart, for the grace of his lips the king shall be his friend. The eyes of the LORD preserve knowledge, and he overthroweth the words of the transgressor.

Today, God is searching for a people who will turn their hearts and beliefs back to the doctrine and teachings of Christ. Sound doctrine is based only in the Word of God. It cannot be theory or opinion. The current church is filled with people who believe different doctrines other than the doctrine of Christ.

Too many times we bend the Gospel to appeal to our personal likes or dislikes. Jesus said,

"My teaching is not mine but comes from the one who sent me. If anyone wants to do his will, he will know whether this teaching is from God or whether I am speaking on my own. The one who speaks on his own seeks his own praise. But the one who seeks the praise of him who sent him is true, and there is nothing false in him." (John 7:16-18)

It is not our job to teach anything except the Word of God. When you truly teach the doctrines of Christ, there will be people who don't want to hear what you say. The Word of God always comes against the acts of the flesh. As we tone down the Gospel to appeal to the masses, we end up teaching doctrines that cause people to applaud us. Feel-good messages that make the people feel happy, but send them to hell. Instead of people moving closer to God, the result is a people moving farther from Him. We need to realize that these are not our words, but these are His Words. Our opinion doesn't matter when it comes to God's Word. While we have gained more understanding of the knowledge of Scripture, be sure that we have also gained more ideologies and thoughts of men. Men have become marketers of the moves of God by taking the principles learned during the different dispensations of God, and then forming denominations. Every denomination formed from the outpouring of God's presence based its formation on a deeper understanding of Scripture revealed by God. Each denomination takes its newfound knowledge and presents it to the masses in order to build a successful organization on the earth. This combination of God's truth and man's agenda will bring forth deadly results. The result is groups filled with doctrines that are from God and doctrines that are from men. The word doctrine comes from the Greek root word *docco* which means "to teach". This word can also mean "what is taught". It's dangerous when men fail to teach God's truth the way He intended it to be taught. Many times we are indoctrinated not only by Scripture, but by what man says is right or wrong. To be a part of the last day Church, every believer must accept the Word of God in its entirety. We must loose ourselves of doctrines and beliefs that are not in accordance with His Word. Our hearts must be in line with the truth of God's

Word. Matthew 15:9 says,

This people draweth nigh unto me with their mouth, and honoureth me with their lips; but their heart is far from me. But in vain they do worship me, teaching for doctrines the commandments of men.

As believers we lose intimacy with God when we depend on the ministers to tell us how to worship. We go through the motions every week, but because God's ordinance is not firmly rooted in our heart, we worship in vain. We fail to touch a personal God because we really have failed to *know* Him. We know what man has taught us *about* Him. We are full of teaching we don't really comprehend because it is based on someone else's experience. The result is religion; having a form of godliness without power. Our hearts are far from God and we believe whatever we're told to. We find ourselves quoting a preacher instead of quoting God's Word. God cannot back up a false belief or a theory developed by a man. Therefore, we must turn to God's Word in order to be a part of His last day bride.

Only those who believe and practice the truth of God's Word will be a part of the last day Church. We have stepped into a time when being involved with the wrong doctrines or beliefs can literally make us a member of a social club instead of the last day Church of Jesus Christ. 1 Timothy 6:3 says,

If any man teach otherwise, and consent not to wholesome words, even the words of our Lord Jesus Christ, and to the doctrine which is according to godliness; He is proud, knowing nothing, but doting about questions and strives of words, whereof cometh envy, strife, railings, evil surmisings, perverse disputings of men of corrupt minds, and destitute of the truth, supposing that gain is godliness: from such withdraw thyself.

Currently, there are many churches, ministers, and members who have turned away from the Scripture and have settled for a man's opinion about Scripture. Many have said that Scripture contradicts itself or that it is not applicable for today. These are teachings that have brought about confusion in the church world. If the Word of God says it you, can believe it. Many corrupt men want to explain away the Scripture they don't like. They want to use vain excuses and say, "It's not for today" or "That was then, this is now"! A true man or woman of God knows that Scripture backs up Scripture. Anyone can take a single Scripture text out of context, but you have a problem when you can't prove what you're saying with other references in God's Word. Many say the gifts of the Holy Spirit are not active today. Jesus said we would do greater works than He had done. He said signs would follow them that believe. The only doctrine I am interested in is the complete infallible Word of God. 2 Timothy 3:16 says,

All scripture is given by inspiration of God, and is profitable for doctrine, for reproof, for correction, for instruction in righteousness: That the man of God may be perfect, thoroughly furnished unto all good works.

By believing the complete Word of God, the man or woman of God will be made perfect and complete in every good work. We are to be perfected by the doctrines of Christ, equipped for a good work. Only the Word of God is able to profit you when you believe. The traditions of men make the Word of God inactive. Every believer has to make a choice, to choose the doctrine of God over the doctrines of men.

I have a problem with preachers who refuse to look at God's Word as the only source and answer to perfect the last day Church. Sound doctrine always returns to the Scripture for guidance. There will be no excuse for those who know what the Word of God says and choose to ignore it. Isaiah 28:9-13 says,

Whom shall he teach knowledge? and whom shall he make to understand doctrine? them that are weaned from the milk, and drawn from the breasts. For precept must be upon precept, precept upon precept; line upon line, line upon line; here a little, and there a little: For with stammering lips and another tongue will he speak to this people. To whom he said, This is the rest wherewith ye may cause the weary to rest; and this is the refreshing: yet they would not hear. But the word of the LORD was unto them precept upon precept, precept upon precept; line upon line, line upon line; here a little, and there a little; that they might go, and fall backward, and be broken, and snared, and taken.

As we grow in Christ by studying the Word, we become responsible for what we know. If we refuse the refreshing and turn away from the meat of God's Word because we refuse to obey it, we will be snared and responsible when we stand before the Lord. It's time for the last day Church to emerge and lay down the false doctrines and ideals of men. Our beliefs will determine where we stand as we continue to approach the return of our Lord. Each of us has a responsibility to continue to find out truth by advancing ourselves in the doctrines of Christ.

Till I come, give attendance to reading, to exhortation, to doctrine. Neglect not the gift that is in thee, which was given thee by prophecy, with the laying on of the hands of the presbytery. Meditate upon these things; give thyself wholly to them; that thy profiting may appear to all. Take heed unto thyself, and unto the doctrine; continue in them: for in doing this thou shalt both save thyself, and them that hear thee. (1 Timothy 4:13-16)

By following the complete Word of God we are able to ensure our salvation as well as those who we are able to minister to. What we believe will either lead people closer to God or away from Him.

In Revelation, John refers to seven churches in existence before the fulfillment of end time events.

Many have thought that these were referenced to certain denominations in existence in the earth. Denominations or church groups like to use these references to point at other organizations that they detest. Some scholars have looked at these churches from a historical sense. I believe that the seven churches exist in every body of believers. Each church represents a doctrine or mindset taught and believed by each individual church member. Our individual beliefs will determine which last day church we belong to. God has begun a search and a separation process to determine who belongs to which church. God will separate those who follow the traditions of men out from those who are real and ready to follow after God. 2 John 1:9-11 says,

For many deceivers are entered into the world, who confess not that Jesus Christ is come in the flesh. This is a deceiver and an antichrist. Look to yourselves, that we lose not those things which we have wrought, but that we receive a full reward. Whosoever transgresseth, and abideth not in the doctrine of Christ, hath not God. He that abideth in the doctrine of Christ, he hath both the Father and the Son. If there come any unto you, and bring not this doctrine, receive him not into your house, neither bid him God speed: For he that biddeth him God

speed is partaker of his evil deeds.

In verse 10 we find the words "look to yourselves." The actual Greek here means "to do an intense inward search into what we believe". It doesn't matter what our past teachings have been. Each of us has full access to the Word of God to study to meet God's approval. If we look internally and separate ourselves from false doctrines taught to us by denomination, family, leader or organization, we will ensure our full reward. Many will find this difficult because we are afraid to leave the comfort of our surroundings and associations. In this same Scripture reference, we find we are not to give false doctrine any place in our house or lives. "God-speed" is a type of encouragement given to those who are doing God's will. We can no longer encourage those who are teaching false doctrine. If we do, we will be counted as partakers of the evil work as it progresses. Encouragement is not given in word only. It can be given in attendance, financial support, and even by association. We must set a guard on our hearts in order to please the Lord.

Our doctrines will determine whether we go with the Lord in the catching away or whether we stay here on the earth. There are people who attend church that will not go in the catching away. God is searching the reigns of the heart. Not every person professing Christ will be caught up to meet Him in the air.

Even thus shall it be in the day when the Son of man is revealed. In that day, he which shall be upon the housetop, and his stuff in the house, let him not come down to take it away: and he that is in the field, let him likewise not return back. Remember Lot's wife. Whosoever shall seek to save his life shall lose it; and whosoever shall lose his life shall preserve it. I tell you, in that night there shall be two men in one bed; the one shall be taken, and the other shall be left. Two women shall be grinding together; the one shall be taken, and the other left. Two men shall be in the field; the one shall be taken, and the other left. And they answered and said unto him, Where, Lord? And he said unto them, Wheresoever the body is, thither will the eagles be gathered together. (Luke 17:30-37)

You notice that in the text we find that each set of individuals appears to be partaking of the same activity. There are many who have the appearance of being owned by Jesus Christ but fail to have the intimacy necessary to be taken with their Lord. Those who fail to have an inward growth with Jesus will not be a part of the bride when He comes. The Holy Spirit was sent to teach us all things. He was sent to reveal to us what has been revealed to Christ. Because of false doctrine, many resist the Holy Spirit and participate in dead works. The disciples wanted to know where this would take place. The last line of this text tells us where. The King James Version poorly translates this line because the accurate translation is "where the dead body is so will the vultures be gathered together." This is also in accordance to the description in Matthew 24:28 where Jesus says, ***"For wheresoever the carcass is, there will the eagles be gathered together".*** A dead body can also be a reference to a dead church, "Where the dead church is so the vultures will gather". As we look at the Greek word for "eagles" or "vultures", we find that its root is *aer* that means "air". The Greek word *aer* also means "to chill or to wax cold". The dead church will resist the truth of God's Word and become cold and dead to the Holy Spirit. It will be lawless. Matthew 24:11-13 says,

And many false prophets shall rise, and shall deceive many. And because iniquity shall abound, the love of many shall wax cold. But he that shall endure unto the end, the same shall be saved.

The Bible reveals that iniquity will cause many in the church to wax cold. This iniquity is a lack of belief in God's true doctrine. In church, we find believers who have mastered the art of appearing sinless; a people able to guard their actions in order to appear pleasing to those around them. Sin and iniquity are two different things. Sin is the actual action that breaks God's law. Iniquity deals with the individual's character to be lawless. Lawlessness is the desire to want nothing to hold us accountable. If we refuse to use the Word of God to come against our beliefs where they are wrong, we will remain full of iniquity. God longs for a people who desire to carry His character and His nature; a people who are so full of Him that they reject anything that doesn't line up with His Word. As we draw close to God, we will remain full of His Spirit, increase in faith, action, and deed in order to bring the fulfillment of the kingdom of God. As you proceed in this book, take the time to really evaluate what you believe. Look at the Scripture given in the text. As we deal with each of these churches, the Scripture given at the very beginning of each chapter contains the truth that will be the answer for those who seek to find it.

Chapter 1

The Hurt Church

For I am persuaded, that neither death, nor life, nor angels, nor principalities, nor powers, nor things present, nor things to come, nor height, nor depth, nor any other creature, shall be able to separate us from the love of God, which is in Christ Jesus our Lord.

Romans 8:38-39

One of the greatest feelings in the world is wrapped up in the moment you receive Christ as your personal Savior. Once you experience the unconditional love of Christ, you find the security and personal peace of knowing you have an intimate relationship with God. Eventually, you grow to understand that the basis of this love is not what He can do for you, but rather what you can do for Him. You long to change the parts of your life He is not pleased with, in order to move closer in relationship to the One you treasure most. Instead of being satisfied with the blessings and gifts He bestows in your life, you find yourself the happiest when you are simply obedient to His will. I believe David understood this moment when He wrote:

"Cast me not away from thy presence; and take not thy holy spirit from me. Restore unto me the joy of thy salvation; and uphold me with thy free spirit." (Psalms 51:11)

The primary goal of the believer should be the increase and development of relationship and intimacy with the Lord. There should be an insatiable hunger to experience more of God's love in our lives each and every day. Longing to keep Him close and near is the very essence of our relationship with Christ.

Early on every believer experiences the true love and power of God at work in their lives. The newborn relationship with God is treasured and intimate in every way. The pursuit of growth causes us to begin to seek out and find a church or organization to help us develop our newfound faith. We soon find ourselves pursuing our faith by practicing the teachings and doctrines of God presented to us by men. Overtime, we slowly become dependent upon a spiritual leader to take us deeper into intimacy with God. Our relationship is slowly replaced by religion. Religion is nothing more than using another man's method to achieve intimacy with the Lord. God never intended for the Church to be filled with duplicate relationships. He designed each of us to have a unique and personal relationship with Him. Looking to our spiritual leader, we depend on his study and fresh word to take us to our next level with God. Idealizing spiritual leadership, we assume that they hold the keys to unlock spiritual truth to help further our growth in Christ. These assumptions cause us to remove our eyes from the Lord and become fixated with spiritual leadership. Because man is fallible, soon we discover the faults and the inadequacies of the leadership we held in such high esteem. Disgusted and hurt, we begin to blame the pastor or the church for allowing us to be taken advantage of. Blaming the leadership, we leave in search of the love we think we have lost because of leadership's lack of commitment to God. But in reality, we lost our intimacy with Christ long ago when we became dependant on someone else to follow through for us. Intimacy with Christ comes by knowing Him through His Word, experiencing Him personally, and walking with Him daily.

There are actually people in our churches who have been hurt so deeply that it seems they will never return to intimacy with Christ again. Inside themselves they ponder the hurt over and over again. Many times they keep the hurt a secret and continue in their meager efforts to find another spiritual representative. While they search for the perfect pastor or church they become great discerners, learning the art of who to trust and who not to. In Revelation 2:1-7 we find a personal letter to these individuals.

Unto the angel of the church of Ephesus write; These things saith he that holdeth the seven stars in his right hand, who walketh in the midst of the seven golden candlesticks; I know thy works, and thy labour, and thy

patience, and how thou canst not bear them which are evil: and thou hast tried them which say they are apostles, and are not, and hast found them liars: And hast borne, and hast patience, and for my name's sake hast laboured, and hast not fainted. Nevertheless I have somewhat against thee, because thou hast left thy first love. Remember therefore from whence thou art fallen, and repent, and do the first works; or else I will come unto thee quickly, and will remove thy candlestick out of his place, except thou repent. But this thou hast, that thou hatest the deeds of the Nicolaitanes, which I also hate. He that hath an ear, let him hear what the Spirit saith unto the churches; To him that overcometh will I give to eat of the tree of life, which is in the midst of the paradise of God.

As we look closely at this Scripture we see a group of people who have been so deeply hurt by false leadership that they spend all of their time looking into church leadership to see if they are good or evil. Obsessed with finding a perfect leader they find themselves evaluating everything they see in church. Instead of focusing on their personal relationship with Christ they become discerners of everyone else. Their personal hurt has caused them to be so cautious that they have become suspicious of everything they see.

The ability to discern good from evil is not only for a few people who move in spiritual gifts, but it is a process of growth experienced by each believer. Many times when we refer to the gift of discernment, we automatically think of the gift of discerning of spirits brought to light in 1 Corinthians 12:10.

To another the working of miracles; to another prophecy; to another discerning of spirits; to another divers kinds of tongues; to another the interpretation of tongues: But all these worketh that one and the self same Spirit, dividing to every man severally as he will.

The gift of discerning of spirits refers to the gift one has to judge prophecy or other spiritual gifts to discern if they are the work of the Holy Spirit or a work of the flesh. God gives the gift of discerning of spirits to man as he wills, but having Godly discernment is the right of every believer. As we grow in the knowledge and wisdom of Christ we should be able to discern good from evil. The individuals who belong to the church of Ephesus have really experienced spiritual growth. The ability to discern good and evil is necessary as we move into the last days.

When wisdom entereth into thine heart, and knowledge is pleasant unto thy soul; Discretion shall preserve thee, understanding shall keep thee: To deliver thee from the way of the evil man, from the man that speaketh froward things; Who leave the paths of uprightness, to walk in the ways of darkness; Who rejoice to do evil, and delight in the frowardness of the wicked; Whose ways are crooked, and they froward in their paths. (Proverbs 2:10-15)

This verse makes reference to the very ones Christ wants us to discern: false apostles, teachers, and preachers who will ultimately be found out. In His letter to the church of Ephesus, the Lord applauds their ability to hate the works of the Nicolaitans. The Nicolaitans were a Gnostic sect in New Testament times, believed to be a result of a proselyte named Nicola added to the church in Acts 6:5. This sect of believers used false doctrines to control the people of God. The Greek word for "Nicolaitans" means "to conquer the people". One of the best descriptions given to us about this type of leader in the New Testament is in 2 Peter 2:12-18. I will reference the New Living Translation for clarity.

These false teachers are like unthinking animals, creatures of instinct, who are born to be caught and

killed. They laugh at the terrifying powers they know so little about, and they will be destroyed along with them. Their destruction is their reward for the harm they have done. They love to indulge in evil pleasures in broad daylight. They are a disgrace and a stain among you. They revel in deceitfulness while they feast with you. They commit adultery with their eyes, and their lust is never satisfied. They make a game of luring unstable people into sin. They train themselves to be greedy; they are doomed and cursed. They have wandered off the right road and followed the way of Balaam son of Beor, who loved to earn money by doing wrong. But Balaam was stopped from his mad course when his donkey rebuked him with a human voice. These people are as useless as dried-up springs of water or as clouds blown away by the wind—promising much and delivering nothing. They are doomed to blackest darkness. They brag about themselves with empty, foolish boasting. With lustful desire as their bait, they lure back into sin those who have just escaped from such wicked living. They promise freedom, but they themselves are slaves to sin and corruption. For you are a slave to whatever controls you. And when people escape from the wicked ways of the world by learning about our Lord and Savior Jesus Christ and then get tangled up with sin and become its slave again, they are worse off than before. (2 Peter 2:12-18 NLT)

As each of us grows in the Lord, we will gain the ability to know the difference between the work of the false and the work of the true. There comes a time in each of our personal walks that we will have to deal with false religion and face it while keeping the right attitude ourselves. In this way, we experience more growth and understanding by realizing the true situation without losing intimacy with the Lord.

Discernment in itself is truly a great attribute, but many who have been hurt in church have become distorted in their judgment. They use the hurt to help them judge who is right and who is wrong. Instead of depending totally on the wisdom attained from the Word of God, they also discern from an emotional experience. The church of Ephesus has become distracted with trying to find a real leader. They have made the search for a true man of God their ultimate concern. Determined to stop the evildoers, they will continue to judge between the real and the false. They spend their time judging men who are in spiritual positions. Consumed with hurt and suspicion, they begin to find fault in everyone they see. Failing to realize their personal walk is suffering, they eventually lose their love for the things of God. They find themselves critical and angry. Unable to satisfy their search for perfection, they eventually quit going to church and decide to stay at home. The Lord is crying out to these individuals with a plea for restoration of their first love. While trying to find a church and true leader they lose true leadership that can only be found by following Jesus, Who is perfect and infallible. The very word "Ephesus" means "desirable ones". Jesus Christ longs and desires the sincere relationship you started out with to be restored. No matter the hurt or the hardness that has developed in your relationship with Christ you are still desirable to Him. His love for you has not changed. It's time to change our mindset and pursue that intimate relationship with God you once held so dear.

O God, don't stay away. My God, please hurry to help me. Bring disgrace and destruction on those who accuse me. May humiliation and shame cover those who want to harm me. But I will keep on hoping for you to help me; I will praise you more and more. I will tell everyone about your righteousness. All day long I will proclaim your saving power, for I am overwhelmed by how much you

have done for me. I will praise your mighty deeds, O Sovereign LORD. I will tell everyone that you alone are just and good. O God, you have taught me from my earliest childhood, and I have constantly told others about the wonderful things you do. Now that I am old and gray, do not abandon me, O God. Let me proclaim your power to this new generation, your mighty miracles to all who come after me. Your righteousness, O God, reaches to the highest heavens. You have done such wonderful things. (Psalms 71:12- 18 NLT)

Turning our minds back to our relationship with God will cause us to continue in the path of righteousness. True restoration will come when we pursue the things of God as we did in the beginning. The Lord longs for us to return to Him by doing the things we did at first. Many times, our relationship suffers because we lose the ability to keep a clear purpose resonating in our walk with Christ. The real purpose of the Church is to press us to experience more of the power of a living God. We should push ourselves to respond to God with the fervor and the hunger as we did in the beginning. If we will repent and turn back to God letting him restore our first love, He has promised to let us eat of the tree of life. Not only will we see heaven, we will begin to experience the life of God's presence in a new and refreshing experience.

And this I pray, that your love may abound yet more and more in knowledge and in all judgment; That ye may approve things that are excellent; that ye may be sincere and without offence till the day of Christ; Being filled with the fruits of righteousness, which are by Jesus Christ, unto the glory and praise of God. (Philippians 1:9-11)

Chapter 2

The Martyred Church

But ye, brethren, are not in darkness, that that day should overtake you as a thief. Ye are all the children of light, and the children of the day: we are not of the night, nor of darkness. Therefore let us not sleep, as do others; but let us watch and be sober. For they that sleep, sleep in the night; and they that be drunken are drunken in the night. But let us, who are of the day, be sober, putting on the breastplate of faith and love; and for a helmet, the hope of salvation. For God hath not appointed us to wrath, but to obtain salvation by our Lord Jesus Christ, Who died for us, that, whether we wake or sleep, we should live together with him.

1 Thessalonians 5:4-10

The twisting of one's belief in Christ and His Word is one of the ultimate tests that each of us as believers will have to face. From the beginning of time the serpent has deceived and beguiled man by reinterpreting the very Word of God to bring forth destruction. When God's law is twisted and used to serve man's agenda it becomes perverted and distorted and the results are catastrophic. Today, we face a multitude of voices representing their motives as divine and their inspirations as pure. New revelation and theologies have become a standard pursuit in the Christian world as we endeavor to gain spiritual knowledge. While the Word of truth is still being proclaimed, many have found themselves being lured into man-made theology by entertainment and hype. The real Gospel of Christ when spoken in truth and power will cause us to deal with the reality of present danger and sin at work in our lives. Anyone can take a portion of the Scripture and use it to make an appealing and interesting theology, but God requires more from those who will be a part of the bride for whom He will return. In John 1:1 we find out that Jesus is the very Word of God spoken and brought into existence in the earth. Therefore, to really know Him and partake of every promise, one has to be able to receive and believe every Scripture in its entirety. Many of the new and old theologies in existence today, have taken pieces of God's Word and used single Scripture references to back up their personal beliefs. Because of the push for new revelation and a desire to become elite in Christendom, many will find themselves following popular fads instead of the truth of God's Word. Many have turned away from the foundational doctrines of the faith and turned to doctrines presented to them by men. The word "deceive" or "beguile" is mentioned in several Scriptures that are centered on the return of Christ and the signs of the end. The specified definition of these words in New Testament context means "to delude the people under pretense of divine inspiration". As new and so-called divine inspiration is unleashed, the people will become easily deluded and believe anything. In Matthew 24:23-27 Jesus said,

"Then if any man shall say unto you, Lo, here is Christ, or there; believe it not. For there shall arise false Christs, and false prophets, and shall show great signs and wonders; insomuch that, if it were possible, they shall deceive the very elect. Behold, I have told you before. Wherefore if they shall say unto you, Behold, he is in the desert; go not forth: behold, he is in the secret chambers;

believe it not. For as the lightning cometh out of the east, and shineth even unto the west; so shall also the coming of the Son of man be."

As much as He was saying, beware of people proclaiming to be Christ, He was also making us aware that there would be men who would say their teachings are from Christ. Every teaching must be scrutinized and refined by the Word of God in order that it would stand as Christ's true doctrine. As the antichrist spirit becomes more and more prevalent, so will teachings that go against what is stated in God's Word. II Thessalonians reveals what causes people to be deceived by the antichrist and receive teachings that are against Christ.

Even him, whose coming is after the working of Satan with all power and signs and lying wonders, And with all deceivableness of unrighteousness in them that perish; because they received not the love of the truth, that they might be saved. And for this cause God shall send them strong delusion, that they should believe a lie: That they all might be damned who believed not the truth, but had pleasure in unrighteousness (2 Thessalonians 2:9-12).

Many will miss the return of Christ for their failure to believe the complete truth of God's Word. Truth is the only asset that one has to remain free from the deception of men. As our society moves farther away from God, we find that all absolutes are being done away with. We no longer want to hear the absolutes in God's Word and become blown about by every wind of doctrine. So we lose the very thing that keeps us free. The apostle makes it very clear early on in this chapter that the Lord's return cannot come until there is a great falling away first. This reference of falling away cannot be made to any other group except pertaining to those within the church. To fall away, one has to have knowledge to fall away from. The movement away from the complete doctrine of Christ will be the demise of many who proclaim to be Christians but are deceived by false teachers.

Many who proclaim to be devout Christians will never receive the promises of God simply because of their unbelief of certain Christian principals and parts of God's Word. Unbelief can keep you from receiving the benefits that have been promised to us as believers. The children of Israel who failed to believe never entered into God's place of rest. Hebrews 3:12-19 gives us a warning while giving an accurate account of their failure.

Take heed, brethren, lest there be in any of you an evil heart of unbelief, in departing from the living God. But exhort one another daily, while it is called today; lest any of you be hardened through the deceitfulness of sin. For we are made partakers of Christ, if we hold the beginning of our confidence steadfast unto the end; While it is said, today if ye will hear his voice, harden not your hearts, as in the provocation. For some, when they had heard, did provoke: howbeit not all that came out of Egypt by Moses. But with whom was he grieved forty years? was it not with them that had sinned, whose carcasses fell in the wilderness? And to whom sware he that they should not enter into his rest, but to them that believed not? So we see that they could not enter in because of unbelief.

I fear that many will miss the catching away of the bride simply because they fail to believe in the complete infallible Word of God. May the Lord soften our hearts to listen to His Word again as we move into these crucial times. You notice that the Word states we will be partakers with Christ "if". This little word is always followed by a condition. The condition is to remain confident in belief from the beginning of our walk with God until the end. Another warning is given to us in Romans 11:20-23.

Thou wilt say then, The branches were broken off, that I might be grafted in. Well; because of unbelief they were broken off, and thou standest by faith. Be not highminded, but fear: For if God spared not the natural branches, take heed lest he also spare not thee. Behold therefore the goodness and severity of God: on them which fell, severity; but toward thee, goodness, if thou continue in his goodness: otherwise thou also shalt be cut off. And they also, if they abide not still in unbelief, shall be grafted in: for God is able to graft them in again.

In this Scripture we find the same thing that happened to physical Israel can also happen to us. If we fail to continue in belief in God's Word, we will be cut off as well. The good news is that anytime you are ready to take Christ at His Word again and apply His will to your life, you can change back into a believer.

In Revelations 2:8 we find a letter to the church of Smyrna.

And unto the angel of the church in Smyrna write;

These things saith the first and the last, which was dead, and is alive; I know thy works, and tribulation, and poverty, (but thou art rich) and I know the blasphemy of them which say they are Jews, and are not, but are the synagogue of Satan. Fear none of those things which thou shalt suffer: behold, the devil shall cast some of you into prison, that ye may be tried; and ye shall have tribulation ten days: be thou faithful unto death, and I will give thee a crown of life. He that hath an ear, let him hear what the Spirit saith unto the churches; He that overcometh shall not be hurt of the second death.

Understanding the meaning of their name can first attain the mindset and the belief system of the church of Smyrna. The word "Smyrna" in Greek means "myrrh". While this tree resin is used in our current culture in many lotions, perfumes, and toiletries, in the times of the early church this smell would have been related with martyrdom or death. Myrrh was burned during Roman funerals to mask the odor emitted by charred and burning corpses. It was said that the Roman Emperor Nero burned a year's worth of myrrh at the funeral of his wife, Poppaea. The early saints who attended the church of Smyrna became very familiar with the idea of being martyred for Christ. Polycarp, the church of Smyrna's presiding bishop was burned at the stake. At eighty-six years of age, he refused to compromise and paid the ultimate price.

Today, there are many churches and denominations that refuse to believe that the book of Revelation is a book of end time events. Many of them hold a strong belief that the events were already fulfilled during the period of the destruction of the Jewish Temple in 70 AD. Some new doctrines even deny the coming and imminent return of Jesus Christ, stating that the Church is Christ so he has already come. I have found that there is also a growing group of believers who believe Christ has called the Church to go through the tribulation. Too many believers in our day have made the assumption that they can hold to such doctrines, and still be caught up with Christ at the catching up of His bride. Because God searches the hearts of men, we need to be made aware that our beliefs can keep us from partaking in certain promises. As Christians, we need to understand how important our beliefs are. In Mark 11:23 it says,

For verily I say unto you, That whosoever shall say unto this mountain, Be thou removed, and be thou cast into the sea; and shall not doubt in his heart, but shall believe that those things which he saith shall come to pass; he shall have whatsoever he saith.

In this passage of Scripture you notice that there are conditions to see the mountain removed. The first and primary condition is that doubt cannot be in your heart. If you doubt the return of Christ or catching away of the bride then you have already made your choice concerning these future events. The belief of the heart is so powerful that when the centurion soldier told Jesus just to speak the word and his servant would be healed it was so. Jesus' response to him can be found in Matthew 8:10-13.

Verily I say unto you, I have not found so great faith, no, not in Israel. And I say unto you, That many shall come from the east and west, and shall sit down with Abraham, and Isaac, and Jacob, in the kingdom of heaven. But the children of the kingdom shall be cast out into outer darkness: there shall be weeping and gnashing of teeth. And Jesus said unto the centurion, Go thy way; and as thou hast believed, so be it done unto thee. And his servant was healed in the selfsame hour.

The centurion was granted his servant's

healing simply by believing that God could do what he had asked. The last statement made by Jesus to the centurion is profound, ***"As thou hast believed, so be it done to thee".*** If you do not believe in the return of Christ or the catching away of the bride you will not find yourself participating in these future promises. What you believe will determine the outcome of your future.

Some of the current doctrines that present a message against the imminent return of Christ and the catching away of the bride can be compared to the doctrines held by the Sadducees. To come against the promise of Jesus' return, is actually coming against the truth of the resurrection. If you do not believe that Christ can return bodily then you must believe the resurrection of our Savior is mere symbolism. If it is all symbolism then you will find there is no hope for the bodily return of Christ. Instead of believing the Word and taking it at what it says, many denominations and doctrines try to rationalize the spiritual accounts in God's Word to no avail. When rational thinking cannot give answer to the spiritual, then the Word of God is said to be false.

As Christians, we are to believe the Word of God above our own rationality. True faith is described as the substance of things hoped for, the evidence of things not seen. The rationalist cannot see how Christ can return, so they spend their time convincing people that the future will not exist. Such doctrine existed in the Sadducees. They denounced the spirit world, refused to believe in the afterlife, and refused to make reference to the teachings of the Prophets or Psalms. They openly rejected the teaching of the resurrection and convinced their followers that there was no future state of punishments or rewards. The Sadducees viewed the law as a moral structure that caused mankind to have the ability to live good lives. In this same way, many preachers in our day have learned to use the Bible as a way to be a helps book that deals with the issues of life. While the Bible holds every answer and key to living a good life in the natural, we need to remember that it also deals with the future state concerning our spiritual walk. The current church system is teaching people to use the Word as a quick fix to the here and now, without focusing on the consequences of the future judgment or work of the Holy Spirit. There is a spirit world that is more real than any natural circumstance we are currently going through. In Acts 23:8, it says that the Sadducees ***"say that there is no resurrection, neither angel, nor spirit: but the Pharisees confess both".*** The rationalist cannot receive the spiritual things of God because they are foolishness to him. The only way to explain away the supernatural work in Scripture is to place it in the past. Many mainline denominations simply use history to explain away events that they don't want to see happen in the future. We have to read the Scripture ourselves and believe what it says over the doctrines of men. Paul addressed this very issue when he wrote in 2 Timothy 2:15-18.

Study to show thyself approved unto God, a workman that needeth not to be ashamed, rightly dividing the word of truth. But shun profane and vain babblings: for they will increase unto more ungodliness. And their word will eat as doth a canker: of whom is Hymenaeus and Philetus; Who concerning the truth have

erred, saying that the resurrection is past already; and overthrow the faith of some.

Here we find Paul coming against two false teachers who were proclaiming that the resurrection had already happened. Religion steals the faith of men by speaking forth questions instead of proclaiming the truth. When we question the Word of God, the end result will always be ungodliness. When we use our intellect to convince people of the fallibility of God's Word we will be responsible for what happens to their faith. The truth is that when we question the Word of God, we are really making room for fallibility to disprove the parts of the Word we don't like. The Sadducees questioned Jesus hoping to solidify their doctrine.

Then came to him certain of the Sadducees, which deny that there is any resurrection; and they asked him, Saying, Master, Moses wrote unto us, If any man's brother die, having a wife, and he die without children, that his brother should take his wife, and raise up seed unto his brother. There were, therefore, seven brethren: and the first took a wife, and died without children. And the second took her to wife, and he died childless. And the third took her; and in like manner the seven also: and they left no children, and died. Last of all the woman died

also. Therefore in the resurrection whose wife of them is she? for seven had her to wife. And Jesus answering said unto them, The children of this world marry, and are given in marriage: But they which shall be accounted worthy to obtain that world, and the resurrection from the dead, neither marry, nor are given in marriage: Neither can they die any more: for they are equal unto the angels; and are the children of God, being the children of the resurrection. Now that the dead are raised, even Moses showed at the bush, when he calleth the Lord the God of Abraham, and the God of Isaac, and the God of Jacob. For he is not a God of the dead, but of the living: for all live unto him (Luke 20:27-38).

To the Sadducees, the natural laws on the earth proved that the resurrection could not exist. Because God is a God of order, they thought that the question of marriage in the afterlife would prove that there was no afterlife. Jesus took their natural question and refuted it by speaking of the difference between the law of the natural and the God of the living. Instead of focusing on their confusion with death, He chose to tell them we live unto God. I am sure that this blew their rational minds. Jesus simply refuted their rational thinking by stating that there is life after death. Through the power of the resurrection, those who believe in Christ never die.

Our rational minds have a hard time understanding how we can live even after death. In the passage of Scripture written to the church of Smyrna in Revelation, Jesus states that He is the first and the last, which was dead but is now alive. It is vital to realize that the resurrection is promised to all who are in Jesus Christ. While the resurrection promise is secure to the believer, we need to realize that our beliefs will determine how we receive resurrection. The church of Smyrna and the church of Philadelphia are the only two churches in the seven who are told that they will receive their crown if they follow through with their instructions. All of the other churches are told specifically to repent or suffer the consequences. To the rationalist, this idea of the two churches reaping the same benefits in different ways seems to be a contradiction. But our beliefs will be what determine which church we belong to. All through Scripture we see the first resurrection demonstrated to us in two ways. Either God catches up the individual or the individual is martyred unto death. Both ways lead to resurrection life eternal. The first resurrection is promised only to those who are in Jesus. Those who are in Christ are partakers of His life, His burial, and His resurrection. Jesus Christ is the firstborn of many brethren. Therefore, the first resurrection makes reference to those who are in Christ Jesus. Those who receive Christ as their Savior carry the same Spirit that raised Christ from the dead and therefore never die. I Corinthians 15:20-24 (NLT) says,

But the fact is that Christ has been raised from the dead. He has become the first of a great harvest of those who will be raised to life again. So you see, just as death came into the world through a man, Adam, now the resurrection from the dead has begun through another man, Christ. Everyone dies because all of us are related to Adam, the first man. But all who are related to Christ, the other man, will be given new life. But there is an order to this resurrection: Christ was raised first; then when Christ comes back, all his people will be raised. After that the end will come, when he will turn the Kingdom over to God the Father, having put down all enemies of every kind.

You notice that the resurrection unto life has an

order to it. First, there is Christ Himself; then there is the resurrection of the bride caught up at His coming, and then the end. The completion of the first resurrection can be found in Revelation 20:4-6.

And I saw thrones, and they sat upon them, and judgment was given unto them: and I saw the souls of them that were beheaded for the witness of Jesus, and for the word of God, and which had not worshipped the beast, neither his image, neither had received his mark upon their foreheads, or in their hands; and they lived and reigned with Christ a thousand years. But the rest of the dead lived not again until the thousand years were finished. This is the first resurrection. Blessed and holy is he that hath part in the first resurrection: on such the second death hath no power, but they shall be priests of God and of Christ, and shall reign with him a thousand years.

Those believers martyred during the tribulation period bring to completion the first resurrection. When Christ addressed the church of Smyrna in Revelation, we must realize that something caused this church to be left behind. Those who stop believing in the return of Christ and the catching away of the bride have made a choice. They have chosen to become martyrs.

Those who choose to receive resurrection in this manner need to understand what they will be up against. The Lord speaks to the church of Smyrna and tells them that to overcome the coming days they must, ***"Fear none of those things which thou shalt suffer"***. The main doctrines that deny the catching away of the bride and the return of Christ base their ideals on the fact that there is no future event that will lead to suffering. The rationalists don't believe in coming tribulation, and some of the other doctrines believe that the Christians on the earth take over and cause future utopia. While these ideas and doctrines are interesting and appealing to the flesh, the Lord told the church of Smyrna that they would suffer. The Scripture in Revelation says that the devil would cast the church of Smyrna into prison to be tried. In the King James translation you find the word "some" inserted into the text, but this word does not occur in the original Greek. This gives us a picture of the early church that suffered great persecution even unto death. In Scripture we find the early disciples spent great amounts of time in prison. I believe that Revelation 12:11 makes reference to the early Church when it states,

And they overcame him by the blood of the Lamb, and by the word of their testimony; and they loved not their lives unto the death.

In Revelation chapter 12 we can see the clear story of Israel, the birth of Jesus Christ, and Lucifer being cast out of heaven to the earth. Because Lucifer was cast into the earth, he made war with the early Church to stop the kingdom of God. The church of Smyrna will have to be ready to face the enemy head on without fear. To reap their reward, they must suffer tribulation for ten days and be faithful unto death. The reference to ten days of tribulation can be compared to Daniel 1:8-15 where Daniel and the three Hebrew boys were faced with defiling themselves with the king's meats and delicacies. Here we find them in a society being tempted, tested, and tried to prove their faithfulness to God. First, they were willing to deny their flesh to the point of fasting for ten days. Eventually, each of them had to choose to trust God completely even to the point of natural death. Whether facing the fiery furnace, or the lion's den; they were willing to stare death in the face. Those who choose to go through the tribulation need to be aware of the types of sacrifices they will have to make for God. If you don't have the mindset to suffer for Christ, you will not make it.

The word "tribulation" in the Greek simply means "to be pressured by affliction or persecution." While the Church deals with tribulation already, as wickedness abounds in the earth, tribulation for those who are in Christ will reach a point of climax. We need to understand that the antichrist spirit is a spirit of selfishness. This spirit is generated by Satan, and will make those who are controlled by it be more concerned with self than the welfare of others. Those who truly follow Christ will be hated simply because they follow God's principles to bring good into the lives of others. The last day tribulation was not made for those who are in Christ, but it was made to bring tribulation on those who are persecutors of Christ and

His work. Those who selfishly justify their own evil works will cause tribulation to come upon the earth. When we think of tribulation, we usually think of God sending famine, earthquakes and other natural disasters. But the truth is that all of these things are the result of wickedness abounding in the earth. The earth was created by God to be governed and ruled by the children of God. The whole earth and the creatures in it cry out to be governed by Godliness. In Romans 8:19-22 it says,

For the earnest expectation of the creature waiteth for the manifestation of the sons of God. For the creature was made subject to vanity, not willingly, but by reason of him who hath subjected the same in hope, Because the creature itself also shall be delivered from the bondage of corruption into the glorious liberty of the children of God. For we know that the whole creation groaneth and travaileth in pain together until now.

All of earth and creation groan to be controlled by the sons of God. As wickedness increases, the earth and God's creation will respond. When the bride is removed from the earth, the natural disasters will increase because of the void of the Godly. We can find this account recorded in Isaiah 24:5-6 where it says,

The earth also is defiled under the inhabitants thereof; because they have transgressed the laws, changed the ordinance, broken the everlasting covenant. Therefore hath the curse devoured the earth, and they that dwell therein are desolate: therefore the inhabitants of the earth are burned, and few men left.

If you choose to go through the tribulation you need to remember that it was your choice. The coming tribulation was not meant for the believer, but it was meant for those who troubled the bride of Christ. By believing the Word of God first and foremost, I will be caught away because I held onto His total Word and believed what I heard as in the beginning. Being a part of the bride of Christ will be my eternal reward.

Seeing it is a righteous thing with God to recompense tribulation to them that trouble you; And to you who are troubled rest with us, when the Lord Jesus shall be revealed from heaven with his mighty angels, In flaming fire taking vengeance on them that know not God, and that obey not the gospel of our Lord Jesus Christ: Who shall be punished with everlasting destruction from the presence of the Lord, and from the glory of his power; When he shall come to be glorified in his saints, and to be

admired in all them that believe (because our testimony among you was believed) in that day (2 Thessalonians 1:6-10)

Chapter 3

The Man Worship Church

Know ye not that they which run in a race run all, but one receiveth the prize? So run, that ye may obtain. And every man that striveth for the mastery is temperate in all things. Now they do it to obtain a corruptible crown; but we an incorruptible. I therefore so run, not as uncertainly; so fight I, not as one that beateth the air: But I keep under my body, and bring it into subjection: lest that by any means, when I have preached to others, I myself should be a castaway.

I Corinthians 9:24-27

As we reflect together on the current state of the overall church, I need to take you back to one of the simple principles revealed to us in God's Word. God is no respecter of persons. This statement simply means that there is not one person above God's judgment. It doesn't matter how long we have been walking with God, or the things we have done for God. Every person will stand before the Lord and give an account for their personal walk with Jesus Christ.

For some reason many of our current day leaders seem to need to be elevated to a place of untouchable authority. This idea of untouchable authority is not new. One of the primary reasons the Jewish leaders hated the work of Jesus is because He questioned their authority and personal walk with God. Instead of focusing on works or traditions, Jesus looked into their hearts. When we look at spiritual leadership in God's Word we need to recognize the differences between the Old and New Testament authority structure. In the Old Testament, the anointing and the work of the Holy Spirit primarily operated in the lives of three types of called individuals. They were the king, prophet, and priest. These men were anointed and used to reveal God's plans to His people. The nation of Israel was called out to be God's nation of promise, but they were unable to govern themselves because disobedience kept them from walking in the Spirit. In the Old Testament the Holy Spirit was reserved for certain individuals in authority, but in Acts Chapter 2 the Holy Spirit was poured out upon all flesh. In the New Testament, Jesus restored man back to God by becoming the final sacrifice for sin. This gave man the ability through Christ to learn to be governed by the Holy Spirit. Today, Jesus gives every individual the opportunity to choose to be obedient to God by obeying His Word and yielding to the Holy Spirit. This means that anyone who yields and obeys will carry the anointing of God as they fulfill His purposes. In Acts 10:34 Peter makes this statement.

Then Peter opened his mouth, and said, Of a truth I perceive that God is no respecter of persons: But in every nation he that feareth him, and worketh righteousness, is accepted with him.

Here, Peter makes it clear that God requires every person to respond to Him with respect and belief. Before we give respect and honor to those in leadership, we need to see leaders fear the Lord and obey His Word by believing it themselves. There is a religious mindset in the church world that demands respect for leadership simply because of title, gift, position, or ability. The respect for the leader cannot be based on talent or ability. The heart and motive of every leader needs to be weighed against God's Word. We fail to realize that our gifts and even our callings are without repentance; meaning that we can operate in an office or spiritual operation even if our heart is wicked. Many in our present-day leadership use their God given gifts and abilities to convince the people that they are above accountability. As the leaders become successful, they choose to believe that monetary gain proves that God has validated their ministry. This idea of validation is dangerous because success and money is not the fruit that God desires. God is not impressed by our ideas of grandeur concerning success and ministry. He is not impressed with the church and its ministries that place emphasis on their personal success over the success of His will and purposes. Every leader and church across America must ask two questions. Who are we? What have we become? Today's church is filled with people who rarely take a close look at who they really are, or who they are following. There are many believers and leaders who play the part of Christianity well but are nothing more than actors playing a role in order to obtain a position of authority. If our heart's desire is seeking authority, blessing, or control, our motive will be revealed when we stand before God. This means that the role of surrendering our hearts to God must remain our primary purpose. While God ultimately knows the heart of every individual, we as believers must be on guard against those in leadership who have wrong motives. If we are not careful, we can end up supporting ministries based on the leaders appeal, talents, and gifts. We must realize that gifts and talents are awesome demonstrations of the power of God at work, but can never replace a true motive and a sincere heart. Instead of focusing on the gifts God has given the leader, we must focus on the leader's fruit and personal walk with God.

Hear what the Lord says to the church of Pergamos in Revelation 2:12-17.

And to the angel of the church in Pergamos write;

These things saith he which hath the sharp sword with two edges; I know thy works, and where thou dwellest, even where Satan's seat is: and thou holdest fast my name, and hast not denied my faith, even in those days wherein Antipas was my faithful martyr, who was slain among you, where Satan dwelleth. But I have a few things against thee, because thou hast there them that hold the doctrine of Balaam, who taught Balac to cast a stumbling block before the children of Israel, to eat things sacrificed unto idols, and to commit fornication. So hast thou also them that hold the doctrine of the Nicolaitanes, which thing I hate. Repent; or else I will come unto thee quickly, and will fight against them with the sword of my mouth. He that hath an ear, let him hear what the Spirit saith unto the churches; To him that overcometh will I give to eat of the hidden manna, and will give him a white stone, and in the stone a new name written, which no man knoweth saving he that recieveth it.

The first reference made in this text to this body of believers is that of Jesus Christ and the two-edged sword. This reference is one that tells us that the Word of God is going to be the final judge, as well as the answer to the problem that this group faces. In Scripture, the two-edged sword can be referenced in Ephesians 6:17 and in Hebrews 4:12. The second of these two references tells us what the two-edged sword will do in verses 12 and 13. It states,

For the word of God is quick, and powerful, and sharper than any two edged sword, piercing even to the dividing asunder of soul and spirit, and of the joints and marrow, and is a discerner of the thoughts and intents of the heart. Neither is there any creature that is not manifest in his sight: but all things are naked and opened unto the eyes of him with whom we have to do.

As we look at this verse, we find that the two-edge sword ultimately judges the inward thoughts, motives and intents of men. When John originally wrote this letter to Pergamos, the very first statement would have been seen as a direct statement to the city governor who was in leadership. The provincial governor alone had power known as "the right of the sword". His position of authority gave him the exclusive power to execute and pass judgment on people who would oppose Caesar in his city. As the letter to Pergamos progresses we see that this group of believers seems to be surrounded by a growing number of false religions. This may be why the reference is given to Pergamos as being where the seat of Satan is. Historically, the city of Pergamos was a city filled with temples to gods of various religions. Within the city walls were temples to Dionysus; the god of wine, Aesclepium; the snake god of healing, Demeter; the goddess of grain, and even a temple to the Roman emperor himself. In fact, Pergamos was the first city to establish an emperor cult. When Christ had John write this letter to Pergamos it seems that He was primarily addressing the idea of man-worship. Anytime people worship the leadership more than they worship Jesus, it will ultimately lead to a place for Satan to sit. As we look into this church, we will find man-worship to be the primary recurring theme. Not only does the letter start by addressing the governing authority of the town, but it also addresses the martyr Antipas. The name "Antipas" is formed from two Greek words, *antee* and *peter*. The name means, "against the father." Many scholars have taken this information and said that this reference is God's way of saying He is against the Pope. While it's easy to relate this to a particular denomination or group, I will take it a step further and say that God is against any leader worship. Apparently, Antipas was considered God's faithful martyr because he refused to involve himself with man-worship and idolatry. In fact, he was willing to suffer death by martyrdom to put a stop to false authority. Too many believers in our day have the mindset that they should never question or oppose a leader in the church setting. What needs to be made clear is that there is a difference between opposing a man obeying infallible Scripture and opposing one who is serving his own motives and agendas. When you oppose a leader who has his actions based on the Word you are not opposing him, you are opposing God. But if the leader's actions are based on self and go against the Word of God then the leader needs to be questioned. Matthew 23:8-12 says,

But be not ye called Rabbi: for one is your Master, even Christ; and all ye are brethren. And call no man your father upon the earth: for one is your Father, which is in heaven. Neither be ye called masters: for one is your Master, even Christ. But he that is greatest among you shall be your servant. And whosoever shall exalt himself shall be abased; and he that shall humble himself shall be exalted.

The religious leaders in Jesus' day wanted respect based on title and position instead of respect based on their ability to follow God's Word. The same thing is happening in our day with many who have obtained a leadership role. True leaders will make every effort to point you to the true master who is Jesus Christ. Instead of making a name or position for self, they will deny self and teach those around them to simply be mastered by Christ. It is impossible to teach others to follow Jesus when we have not learned to follow Him ourselves. True leadership must decide to follow God above self. Too many ministers find themselves in a quandary. How can a leader be led? To be led seems to be a place of vulnerability in leadership. Because if we are led then that means someone else might have the answer to the problem. In the "self" mindset this would mean that if someone else had the answer then they would be questioning our authority. Too many leaders have a longing for absolute power. There are congregations across our country who have been taught to worship the man of God as the final authority. This is idolatry and God will not tolerate it. There is only one head of the Church and that is Jesus Christ. The churches and the leaders with this type of mindset will lead God's people into destruction.

As Jesus continues in His efforts to speak to Pergamos, we find that he begins to address specific doctrines held by the church itself. The first doctrine He addresses is the doctrine of Balaam. This doctrine is discovered and identified by looking into the story of Balaam in Numbers 22. Here we find that King Balak sent messengers to the prophet Balaam to have him use his prophetic gift to curse the nation of Israel. King Balak needed someone with a spiritual gift to control Israel because of the sheer number of God's people who had moved into Moab. Apparently, Balaam was quite accurate with his prophetic gifting. In Numbers 22:6 King Balak tells Balaam, ***"I wot that he whom thou blesseth is blessed, and he whom thou curseth is cursed".*** A few verses later we see that King Balak sent his messengers with the rewards of divination in their hand. Every self-motivated leader or authority that has a desire for control and power seems to have a price. The first time the messengers came, Balaam listened to the Lord's council and turned them away. King Balak continued to send princes and men of honor to Balaam to get him to give in. Finally, in Numbers 22:15-22 we find Balaam's selling price.

Thus saith Balak the son of Zippor, Let nothing, I pray thee, hinder thee from coming unto me: For I will promote thee unto very great honor, and I will do whatsoever thou sayest unto me: come therefore, I pray thee, curse me this people. And Balaam answered and said unto the servants of Balak, If Balak would give me his house full of silver and gold, I cannot go beyond the word of the LORD my God, to do less or more. Now therefore, I pray you, tarry ye also here this night, that I may know what the LORD will say unto me more. And God came unto Balaam at night, and said unto him, If the men come to call thee, rise up, and go with them; but yet the word which I shall say unto thee, that shalt thou do. And Balaam rose up in the morning, and saddled his ass, and went with the princes of Moab. And God's anger was kindled because he went: and the angel of the LORD stood in the way for an adversary against him.

Power hungry spiritual authority is more than willing to sell their gift when it means more honor. It's amazing that Balaam held out until Balak said that he would promote Balaam unto very great honor. Along with this great honor He also let Balaam set his own price for his services. I believe that when Balaam continued to entertain the offers and then named his price, this let God know Balaam's heart. In the Word we find God then telling Balaam to do what He told him not to do before. Sometimes we fail to realize that the condition of our heart will determine what instructions God will give to us. When Balaam's heart was right God tried to keep him from danger. A few verses later we see that God's anger was kindled against Balaam and God sent forth an angel to his destruction. It was not God who changed, but rather Balaam who changed. Balaam's wicked heart had made him blind to coming judgment.

In Numbers 22:22-33, the story gives us further insight into Balaam's doctrine.

Now he was riding upon his ass, and his two servants were with him. And the ass saw the angel of the LORD standing in the way, and his sword drawn in his hand: and the ass turned aside out of the way, and went into the field: and Balaam smote the ass, to turn her into the way. But the angel of the LORD stood in a path of the vineyards, a wall being on this side, and a wall on that side. And when the ass saw the angel of the LORD, she thrust herself unto the wall, and crushed Balaam's foot against the wall: and he smote her again. And the angel

of the LORD went further, and stood in a narrow place, where was no way to turn either to the right hand or to the left. [27]And when the ass saw the angel of the LORD, she fell down under Balaam: and Balaam's anger was kindled, and he smote the ass with a staff. And the LORD opened the mouth of the ass, and she said unto Balaam, What have I done unto thee, that thou hast smitten me these three times? And Balaam said unto the ass, Because thou hast mocked me: I would there were a sword in mine hand, for now would I kill thee. And the ass said unto Balaam, Am not I thine ass, upon which thou hast ridden ever since I was thine unto this day? was I ever wont to do so unto thee? And he said, Nay. Then the LORD opened the eyes of Balaam, and he saw the angel of the LORD standing in the way, and his sword drawn in his hand: and he bowed down his head, and fell flat on his face. And the angel of the LORD said unto him, Wherefore hast thou smitten thine ass these three times? behold, I went out to withstand thee, because thy way is perverse before me: And the ass saw me, and turned from me these three times: unless she had turned from me, surely now also I had slain thee, and saved her alive.

Balaam's blindness caused his spiritual insight to fail, he could not see the impending judgment of God. The servants of Balaam could not see what was coming either. When spiritual leadership starts to use its gifts for gain, the only thing standing between them and God's judgment is the "ass" that is carrying them. The word for "ass" in Hebrew simply means "to continue with persistence and patience". I believe that the church that holds onto the Word of God is the only thing that can stop God's judgment from coming to wicked and controlling leadership. Balaam's ass was the one who saw what was coming. It responded appropriately by turning aside to stop the impending doom. But when it did, Balaam smote the ass to make her go his direction. The next move the ass took was to crush Balaam's foot into the wall. Balaam's' response was to smite the ass again. When the way got so narrow that the end was drawing near, the ass simply stopped all support and fell underneath him. Balaam smote her with his staff. The staff in Scripture has always represented authority and leadership. Balaam used his position of power to bring self-motivated correction. The ass saw the angel and took immediate action to prevent Balaam's demise. Too many pastors and leaders fail to take heed to correction sent to them by their own congregations. The ass was thinking of Balaam's welfare, but all he could do was continue to beat her until she did what he wanted. Balaam not only used his gifts to get money, but he beat the very beast that was giving him support and love. God made the ass speak. Be sure that God will send warning to leadership through their congregations before His judgment comes. When the ass spoke she told Balaam that she was his ass and had never gone against him before. It is amazing what leadership will put their congregations through when it comes to personal wants and wishes.

The doctrine of man-worship is dangerous because if the congregation believes in this type of theology there will be no one to give the leadership warnings to stop the coming judgment. In Greek, the very name "Pergamos" means "to elevate, to tower", it also means "height". If church leadership towers above the people to the point that they fail to receive God's sent warnings, then they have started practicing the doctrine of Balaam. In Hebrew, Balaam's name means, "not of the people". When the church leadership separates themselves from the people, they are in grave danger. Basically, they are refusing to allow God access to question their authority or actions. Instead of appreciating the congregation, who are the support and backbone of their ministry, they abuse their position of authority and beat the sheep to fulfill their desires. Every believer has a responsibility to learn to only support leadership who is following after God. The fruit and the heart of the leader reveal this. You notice that the ass fell underneath Balaam to stop the judgment to come. The only way to stop the progression of power and authority abuse in leadership is for the people of God to stop financing and supporting ministers and ministries who use their gifts to benefit self. When the ass stopped its support, Balaam repented and got further instruction from the Lord.

The Lord then used Balaam to bless Israel and turned the tables on King Balak. Three times Balak tried to get Balaam to prophesy Israel's destruction and three times Balaam spoke only blessing. The fourth prophesy that came forth actually spoke forth the coming of the Messiah, and Moab's impending destruction. The letter written to the church of Pergomos in Revelation 2:14 reads Balaam "***taught Balak to cast a stumbling block before the children of Israel, to eat things sacrificed unto idols, and to commit fornication"***. When Balaam's prophesies failed to give Balak his desired outcome, Balaam gave King Balak a different strategy. This strategy is recorded in the historical books of Josephus, Philo, and in the Samaritan book of Joshua. In these accounts it is said that Balaam told Balak to get the daughters of the Midianites to fornicate with the young men of Israel. By doing this, the young men would be led into idolatry to other gods, and this would destroy Israel. Apparently, this plan was executed. In Numbers 25:1 it says,

And the people began to commit whoredom with the daughters of Moab. And they called the people unto the sacrifices of their gods: and the people did eat, and bowed down to their gods. And Israel joined himself unto Baalpeor: and the anger of the LORD was kindled against Israel.

The Lord then informed Israel to slay all of the men that had joined themselves to the women of

Moab. In verse 9 it says that they destroyed 24,000 men. Later in Numbers 31 when Israel went in to destroy Moab, the people tried to save the Moabite women and Moses said in verse 15,

"Have ye saved all the women alive? Behold, these caused the children of Israel, through the counsel of Balaam, to commit trespass against the LORD in the matter of Peor, and there was a plague among the congregation of the LORD".

If Balaam could not use his gift to get Balak what he wanted, then he used the lust of the people to get Balak what he wanted. In Hebrew, Balak's name means "devastator". Satan has a desire to devastate the kingdom of God through wicked leadership and selfish desire. Self-motivated leaders will control the people either through their gifts and authority, or by telling the people what they want to hear so that they are inspired by lust.

The church of Pergamos is a group of believers that believe spiritual leadership is untouchable and answers to no one. This church group find themselves worshiping the man more than the Lord who gave the man the authority and gift. Simply stated, this is the church that allows and empowers abuse and manipulation by church leadership. In Revelation 2:15 Jesus says, ***"So hast thou also them that hold the doctrine of the Nicolaitanes, which thing I hate".*** The word "Nicolations" is formed from two Greek root words, *nikao* which means "to conquer" and *laos* which means "the people". It's time for all of us to understand that it is wrong for leadership to conquer God's people. The doctrine of the Nicolations simply represents the hierarchy of a ruling class over the rest of the people. One thing God cannot stand is spiritual elitism. Our acceptance of such nonsense has created men and women of God who look more like celebrities than servants. I believe that the people of God allow this because they too have a desire to be celebrities. The church of Pergamos is deceived in their thinking. They believe if God gives wealth and celebrity status to the man or woman of God then eventually, He will give it to them. The only thing coming to this group of believers is God's impending judgment unless they wake up and repent of these evil beliefs. In Revelation 2:16 Jesus Himself says, ***"Repent; or else I will come unto thee quickly, and will fight against them with the sword of my mouth".*** The Scripture false leadership has used to manipulate and fulfill selfish desires will be the very sword that destroys them if they fail to turn away from these man-made doctrines.

I want to stop and speak directly to leaders who may be reading this book. All of us need to remember that each of us has the potential to abuse the authority God has given to us and use it for personal gain. The Holy Spirit wants those in authority to evaluate ourselves and consider that we will not just be judged on our ability to preach or divide the Word, but we will primarily be judged on how we treat God's sheep. Ezekiel chapter 34 speaks directly to the shepherds of God's sheep. In verses 7-10 the Lord says,

"Therefore, ye shepherds, hear the word of the LORD; As I live, saith the Lord GOD, surely because my flock became a prey, and my flock became meat to every beast of the field, because there was no shepherd, neither

did my shepherds search for my flock, but the shepherds fed themselves, and fed not my flock; Therefore, O ye shepherds, hear the word of the LORD; Thus saith the Lord GOD; Behold, I am against the shepherds; and I will require my flock at their hand, and cause them to cease from feeding the flock; neither shall the shepherds feed themselves anymore; for I will deliver my flock from their mouth, that they may not be meat for them".

As leaders we need to understand that these are not our sheep to do with as we please. We must get the idea of "my sheep" out of our minds. Instead, we need to realize that the Church and its members are God's property. In Ezekiel 34:20-24 the Lord directs His attention to the flock itself and says,

"Therefore thus saith the Lord GOD unto them; Behold, I, even I, will judge between the fat cattle and between the lean cattle. Because ye have thrust with side and with shoulder, and pushed all the diseased with your horns, till ye have scattered them abroad; Therefore will I save my flock, and they shall no more be a prey; and I will judge between cattle and cattle. And I will set up one shepherd over them, and he shall feed them, even my servant David; he shall feed them, and he shall be their shepherd. And I the LORD will be their God, and my servant David a prince among them; I the LORD have spoken it".

The Lord is not pleased with the members of the flock who have more substance and abuse those who lack. Money may have been able to buy off the local pastor or minister, but the Lord says that Jesus Christ will be the one Shepherd who will not be bought. In Acts 20:28-30 the Apostle Paul gives a warning to the leaders and members of the early church. He says,

"Take heed therefore unto yourselves, and to all the flock, over the which the Holy Ghost hath made you overseers, to feed the church of God, which he hath purchased with his own blood. For I know this, that after my departing shall grievous wolves enter in among you, not sparing the flock. Also of your own selves shall men arise, speaking perverse things, to draw away disciples after them. Therefore watch, and remember, that by the space of three years I ceased not to warn every one night and day with tears. And now, brethren, I commend you to God, and to the word of his grace, which is able to build you up, and to give you an inheritance among all them which are sanctified. I have coveted no man's silver, or gold, or apparel. Yea, ye yourselves know, that these hands have ministered unto my necessities, and to them that were with me. I have showed you all things, how that so laboring ye ought to support the weak, and to remember the words of the Lord Jesus, how he said, It is more blessed to give than to receive".

You notice that this Scripture does not seem to indicate that the wolves would come in from outside the church, but rather from those who were inside the fellowship. Paul then goes on to talk about coveting silver, gold, and apparel. I think that the Lord let Paul know that the wolves would be the leaders who would covet after the things of the world. He gave heed to let the church know that the very leaders that were called to oversee the flock have the potential to devour the flock for selfish gain. These leaders not only have a hunger for material wealth, but they also have the ability to build a faithful following. Be aware that every leader has the ability to disciple God's flock into their image. While these leaders can be quite convincing, not one of them can give eternal life to their followers. In Revelation 2:17 Jesus tells the church of Pergamos,

"To him that overcometh will I give to eat of the hidden manna, and will give him a white stone, and in the stone a new name written, which no man knoweth saving he that receiveth it."

For those who repent of this belief system, Jesus Christ says He will give them hidden manna. In the

Greek, the word for "hidden" means "to give a secret or hidden escape notice". The word for "manna" simply means "a miraculous gift". Jesus says that He will give each of them that repent a white stone. In the ancient courts of justice, the accused were condemned by black pebbles and acquitted by white. These pebbles represented votes from the accusers. Jesus is letting us know that if we repent of these false beliefs, he will acquit us and give us His name. He will choose us and we will be His prize possession. The final statement of the text lets us know that Jesus alone has the power to know those who are His. There is not one leader who has the power or authority to give a follower eternal life. Jesus is the only Shepherd who has this level of power and authority.

Chapter 4

The Big Business Church

The preparations of the heart in man, and the answer of the tongue, is from the LORD. All the ways of a man are clean in his own eyes; but the LORD weigheth the spirits. Commit thy works unto the LORD, and thy thoughts shall be established. The LORD hath made all things for himself: yea, even the wicked for the day of evil. Every one that is proud in heart is an abomination to the LORD: though hand join in hand, he shall not be unpunished. By mercy and truth iniquity is purged: and by the fear of the LORD men depart from evil. When a man's ways please the LORD, he maketh even his enemies to be at peace with him. Better is a little with righteousness than great revenues without right. A man's heart deviseth his way: but the LORD directeth his steps.

Proverbs 16:1-9

In our times, most believers know that God loved them even while they were destitute and broken in their sin. This thought sustains us in our walk with God and lets us know that God is serious about His relationship with us. It's awesome to know that God pursues us and longs for us even when we lack His state of perfection. He called us to be a part of His Church when we were the ones in desperate need of someone to love us and forgive us. Jesus did that for each of us. He called to us and longed for us even when we failed to realize that we had a longing for Him. This initial drawing is God's way of pursuing us until we become passionate about Him. As we develop a true love for Jesus, there are tests that will come to prove our passion. In the church world, we say that we have given God our whole heart, yet within the heart, we find pleasure in other places, people, and things. On Sundays, churches are filled with people who are despondent and destitute of passion for the Jesus they say they love. Many people sit through the Sunday service with boredom and disdain. They can't wait to fill their bellies with food after the service. The idea of Sunday service being over brings great excitement as they anticipate what they will do after the torture stops.

Humanity loves the idea that God loves them, but they detest the idea of committing to a relationship that will require them to truly love the Lord and change for His benefit. True heartfelt love for Jesus is the only thing that will produce a combination of passion and commitment to the things of God. To have Jesus love us with an everlasting love, but deny our responsibility to nurture and grow the relationship on our own creates a group of churched people who are using the Lord for selfish reasons.

Many of us think that God is not aware of how we truly feel about Him, but what we do not know is that our heart is demonstrated in our words, actions, and deeds. To get an accurate view of our heart's desire, we must look to the things in our lives that cause us to be passionate and committed. Whatever these things are, they hold our true heart's affections. Jeremiah 17:9-11 says,

The heart is deceitful above all things, and desperately wicked: who can know it? I the LORD search the heart, I try the reins, even to give every man

according to his ways, and according to the fruit of his doings. As the partridge sitteth on eggs, and hatcheth them not; so he that getteth riches, and not by right, shall leave them in the midst of his days, and at his end shall be a fool.

This powerful Scripture reveals that the only person who truly knows our heart is the Lord. This means that our heart can deceive us into thinking that we really love the Lord, but in reality, the fruit of our doings tell a different story.

The true bride of Christ is going to be revealed as we approach the coming of the Lord. This bride will be moved with passion for the one she loves. She will be mature and grown to the stature of Christ. Her love and passion for God will be so intimate that it will keep her from falling prey to the ideals and ways of the world. She will be totally committed to Christ through His Word and Spirit. Many times, when we counsel those who are to be married we tell each person that it is important that they both serve the Lord because Christ does not want the couple unequally yoked. This Scripture reference is found in

2 Corinthians 6:14-18 and says,

Be ye not unequally yoked together with unbelievers: for what fellowship hath righteousness with unrighteousness? and what communion hath light with darkness? And what concord hath Christ with Belial? or what part hath he that believeth with an infidel? And what agreement hath the temple of God with idols? for ye are the temple of the living God; as God hath said, I will dwell in them, and walk in them; and I will be their God, and they shall be my people. Wherefore come out from among them, and be ye separate, saith the Lord, and touch not the unclean thing; and I will receive you, and will be a Father unto you, and ye shall be my sons and daughters, saith the Lord Almighty.

As you can see this verse makes no reference to marriage or two people becoming one flesh, but the word for "unequally yoked" in Greek actually means "to fornicate or have intimacy with idolaters". The last line of this text reveals that God will not accept or receive a church that has come into agreement with the world. How do I know this Scripture meant the Church? Paul wrote this letter to the Corinthians that was a body of believers; therefore, every body of believers needs to heed this writing. The only reference to marriage given in this Scripture would have to be from God to His bride. The bride of Christ has to choose to love Christ alone. Jesus will not marry a group of people who are not willing to make a full commitment to Him by following His teachings and the Holy Spirit. In Ephesians chapter 4 there is a verse that says that the Church has to come into the full measure and stature of Christ. This simply means that Jesus cannot and will not marry a people who refuse to grow to His level by becoming mature. As our High Priest, Levitical law places limits on Jesus Christ on who He can marry. Remember, Jesus did not come to do away with the law, but to fulfill the law. In Leviticus 21:10-15 it says,

And he that is the high priest among his brethren, upon whose head the anointing oil was poured, and that is consecrated to put on the garments, shall not uncover his head, nor rend his clothes; Neither shall he go into any dead body, nor defile himself for his father, or for his mother; Neither shall he go out of the sanctuary, nor profane the sanctuary of his God; for the crown of the anointing oil of his God is upon him: I am the LORD. And he shall take a wife in her virginity. A widow, or a divorced woman, or profane, or an harlot, these shall he not take: but he shall take a virgin of his own people to wife. Neither shall he profane his seed among his people:

for I the LORD do sanctify him.

This Scripture not only reveals who Jesus must marry, but it also reveals who He cannot marry. To be the bride of Christ we must make a declaration in our hearts to Him alone. You cannot fulfill the lusts of the flesh and expect to be caught up to be with the Lord. You cannot make agreements with the world and expect to be the bride of Christ. Jesus Christ will not be joined to a harlot. He cannot be joined to someone who is married to another, or to someone who is footloose and fancy-free. He must only marry a virgin who has been kept for Him alone. He will not share His bride with the world. He will not share you with your own fleshly desires. The true bride desires Him alone. Nothing else satisfies for only He can bring fulfillment. You may say how can I be a virgin when I was corrupt before I received the Lord. The Apostle Paul reveals this to us in 2 Corinthians 11:2-4,

"For I am jealous over you with godly jealousy: for I have espoused you to one husband, that I may present you as a chaste virgin to Christ. But I fear, lest by any means, as the serpent beguiled Eve through his subtlety, so your minds should be corrupted from the simplicity that is in Christ. For if he that cometh preacheth

another Jesus, whom we have not preached, or if ye receive another spirit, which ye have not received, or another gospel, which ye have not accepted, ye might bear well with him".

Paul tells the Corinthian church that all the teachings he had given them were given to fulfill one purpose. That purpose was to present them as a body of believers as a chaste or pure virgin to Jesus Christ. He then goes on to say that there will be other ministers who will come unto them preaching another kind of Jesus, with the wrong spirit, and false good news. He reminds them that this is not the God they have accepted and tells them that they have to learn to bear with them. This simply means that they will have to stay chaste and pure even in the midst of false teaching. Most of the false teaching is teaching that tickles our ears or gratifies our fleshly desires. It is teaching that tells us what we want to hear instead of what is required of us to be the bride of Christ. This is the choice each of us will have to make.

Now that we know what kind of bride Jesus will

marry, all of us need to be made aware of the harlot church. I like to refer to her as the runaway bride. The runaway bride gets nervous at the idea of true commitment to the things of God. Standing at the altar she starts to get cold feet and thinks about all the things in this life she will miss out on if she makes a commitment of marriage. She needs to hear that she can have Jesus and still be able to live her life in the now. The idea of Jesus is an idea of the future that only comes on the Day of Judgment or the moment someone dies. The runaway bride makes everything else more important than her relationship with Jesus Christ. She has a deep desire to run after and acquire things. These things become the driving force that governs her life. To appease these types of desires and bring numbers into a building, the local church preaches on topics that appeal to the wants and desires of the people instead of the wants and desires of God. The ministers preach sermons that fulfill the runaway bride's desire to lust after the temporal in this life. While the Word of God clearly states that those who serve the Lord will reap certain benefits and blessings, we need to be aware that the benefits and blessings are not the reasons we serve the Lord. The runaway bride is only motivated to serve God when God fulfills her wants and wishes. This is what makes her a harlot; her heart is not after a true relationship with God; her heart is after the blessings God's people possess. Churches that yield to the runaway bride give fewer altar calls, preach messages that evolve around man's goodness and personal success, water down the Word to avoid offense, and focus on building a worldly kingdom instead of an eternal one. The runaway bride has no intention of ever marrying; she simply wants to be wined and dined like someone on a date. The runaway bride will be enticed with false doctrine because it's not commitment to the truth she is after, rather it is the "things" that she desires to possess. The more enticing things the doctrine promises, the more open and willing she is to receive it. Proverbs 30:20 tells us about this runaway when it says, ***Such is the way of an adulterous woman; she eateth, and wipeth her mouth, and saith, I have done no wickedness.***

The dangerous thing about the appeasement of the runaway bride is that she grows in great numbers. The idea that God is going to fulfill our earthly desires appeals to the masses, churched or un-churched. It's great to know that all of humanity can come together united with the common ground of selfish gain. I fear that the American church has produced and mothered a group of church people who are in it for all the wrong reasons. The teachings coming across many pulpits seem to be focused on self. I think that this has become possible because the various denominations, organizations, and even local bodies are motivated by selfish gain instead of the reality of our relationship with Jesus. Someone with a true relationship with Christ doesn't have to have things to make them go to church. There is only one thing that they desire and that is to have a life-changing experience in Christ through the work of the Holy Spirit, so that they will be pleasing to Jesus by lining up with His Word. You can have things at your church, but if lives are not being transformed to measure up to the image of Jesus Christ, then all of it is in vain. In the Old Testament, Israel's leaders became guilty of mothering the people to sin instead of leading them to a relationship with God. Hosea 2:2-5 says,

Plead with your mother, plead: for she is not my wife, neither am I her husband: let her therefore put away her whoredoms out of her sight, and her adulteries from between her breasts; Lest I strip her naked, and set her as in the day that she was born, and make her as a wilderness, and set her like a dry land, and slay her with thirst. And I will not have mercy upon her children; for they be the children of whoredoms. For their mother hath played the harlot: she that conceived them hath done shamefully: for she said, I will go after my lovers, that give me my bread and my water, my wool and my flax, mine oil and my drink.

As we approach the coming of the Lord, every church and organization without pure motives will be revealed for what they are. The word "harlot" in Hebrew means "highly fed and therefore wanton." The harlot church is never satisfied because there is always the bigger and better. She has tasted of the things of the world and now wants more of it, all in the name of Christ, of course. The sad fact is that all of the people following these types of teachings will be cut off as well. The harlot church is more interested in lovers than the One true love. The runaway bride will come into agreement with anything that gives it the earthly possessions it desires. This not only happens to individuals, but it happens to whole churches, assemblies, and organizations when the desire for success outweighs the desire for God. It's time that the Church remembers that God's doesn't require large crowds to move or show up. He doesn't require lights, fireworks, and a television show to do His work. Hollywood requires these things, entertainer's need a big production to perform, and stars are never satisfied until they see their names in lights. God only requires one thing to show up and perform in a powerful way. That one thing is a sincere and pure motivation from the heart. The great thing about God is that it is never about the masses; it's all about dealing with one heart at a time.

In Proverbs 7, we find a sincere warning from the Lord to those who are enticed to join themselves with the runaway bride. It's easy to think that we are serving the Lord for the right reasons when in reality we are serving the desires of the flesh. Many who are motivated by these types of teachings may be succumbing to them unaware. Proverbs 7:1-23 says,

My son, keep my words, and lay up my commandments with thee. Keep my commandments, and live; and my law as the apple of thine eye. Bind them upon thy fingers, write them upon the table of thine heart. Say unto wisdom, Thou art my sister; and call understanding thy kinswoman: That they may keep thee from the strange woman, from the stranger which flattereth with her words. For at the window of my house I looked through my casement, And beheld among the simple ones, I discerned among the youths, a young man void of understanding, Passing through the street near her corner; and he went the way to her house, In the twilight, in the evening , in the black and dark night: And, behold, there met him a woman with the attire of an harlot, and subtle of heart. (She is loud and stubborn; her feet abide not in her house: Now is she without, now in the streets, and lieth in wait at every corner.) So she caught him, and kissed him, and with an impudent face said unto him, I have peace offerings with me; this day have I payed my vows. Therefore came I forth to meet thee, diligently to seek thy face, and I have found thee. I have decked my bed with coverings of tapestry, with carved works, with fine linen of Egypt. I have perfumed my bed with myrrh, aloes, and cinnamon. Come, let us take our fill of love until the morning: let us solace

ourselves with loves. For the goodman is not at home, he is gone a long journey: He hath taken a bag of money with him, and will come home at the day appointed. With her much fair speech she caused him to yield, with the flattering of her lips she forced him. He goeth after her straightway, as an ox goeth to the slaughter, or as a fool to the correction of the stocks; Till a dart strike through his liver; as a bird hasteth to the snare, and knoweth not that it is for his life.

The only thing that preserves you from the runaway bride is to know the commandments of God yourself. God's commandments cannot just be something we talk about occasionally. As believer's we must have the Word of God at our fingertips and then have the Holy Spirit write them upon our hearts. This means we must love the commandments of God. The harlot church's only ability is the ability to flatter people with words. The word "flattereth" means "to use smooth talk to take away your portion". The only person who will succumb to the runaway bride is the one who is void of understanding. In Hebrew, to be "void of understanding" is defined as "one without heart or will to remain centered ". This text of Scripture is very prophetic because it says that this woman would be on every corner. You and I know that one woman can't be on every corner, but in this hour it seems that churches are on every corner. The runaway bride is not only good at fair speeches, but she also gives offerings and pays her vows. The harlot church tells the one who lacks the ability to remain centered on Christ to come and be fulfilled with loves. The only thing that could keep the young man from giving in, is his knowledge that Christ would soon return. But the runaway bride tells him that the good man is on a journey and will return someday. The moment the individual yields his will to the desire for loves, the Scripture says she forces him. In Hebrew this means, "to be banished by compelling ". Yielding to the harlot church will banish you from being a part of the bride of Christ. Those who are a part of the runaway bride fail to realize that what will be required of you is your life. Without the ability to recognize the false bride, many people will continue to fall prey to false teachings. They will serve the Lord for things instead of for a sincere relationship with Christ. While at times it can seem confusing and mind-boggling to figure out what is real and what is not, Proverbs 23:27 gives us the key to identify the true bride from the false.

For a whore is a deep ditch; and a strange woman is a narrow pit. She also lieth in wait as for a prey, and increaseth the transgressors among men.

The last line of this Scripture gives us the key to recognize the runaway bride. No matter what she teaches or does, be sure that she will increase transgressions among men. Being a part of the true bride will cause sin to decrease in your life not increase. The true bride of Christ will preach the complete Word of God bringing change to the hearer. The runaway bride will cause sin to increase. It will make room for more sin and less room for real change. Identifying the harlot church will get easier as we approach the coming of the Lord.

In Revelation 2:18-29, Jesus speaks directly to the runaway bride.

"And unto the angel of the church in Thyatira write; God, who hath These things saith the Son of his eyes like unto a flame of fire, and his feet are like fine brass; I know thy works, and charity, and service, and faith, and

thy patience, and thy works; and the last to be more than the first. Notwithstanding I have a few things against thee, because thou sufferest that woman Jezebel, which calleth herself a prophetess, to teach and to seduce my servants to commit fornication, and to eat things sacrificed unto idols. And I gave her space to repent of her fornication; and she repented not. Behold, I will cast her into a bed, and them that commit adultery with her into great tribulation, except they repent of their deeds. And I will kill her children with death; and all the churches shall know that I am he which searcheth the reins and hearts: and I will give unto every one of you according to your works. But unto you I say, and unto the rest in Thyatira, as many as have not this doctrine, and which have not known the depths of Satan, as they speak; I will put upon you none other burden. But that which ye have already hold fast till I come. And he that overcometh, and keepeth my works unto the end, to him will I give power over the nations: And he shall rule them with a rod of iron; as the vessels of a potter shall they be broken to shivers: even as I received of my Father. And I will give him the morning star. He that hath an ear, let him hear what the Spirit saith unto the churches."

As we look into this letter to the church of Thyatira we find that the word Thyatira has little or no meaning to gain understanding from in the Greek. To understand this church and her doctrine we must look to historical reference to tell what she believes and who she is. The first reference we can look to in Scripture is found in Acts 16:14-15 where Scripture gives reference to a woman named Lydia.

And a certain woman named Lydia, a seller of purple, of the city of Thyatira, which worshipped God, heard us: whose heart the Lord opened, that she attended unto the things which were spoken of Paul. And when she was baptized, and her household, she besought us, saying, If ye have judged me to be faithful to the Lord, come into my house, and abide there. And she constrained us.

In this reference, Scripture tells us that Lydia was a seller of purple. As we research Thyatira, we find that the people of the city gained their living by traffic and the art of dying cloth purple. This business of trading and dying this purple cloth was quite lucrative and brought wealth to the merchants of the city from around the world. The merchants and businessmen of Thyatira gathered together and formed trade unions that kept the price high and the merchants and workers loyal. To continue to be a part of this profiting industry, the workers and merchants had to participate in the unions by coming to the guild meetings. During these gatherings there would be pagan worship, discussion of trade matters, a business dinner, and then ritual orgies. Not to join a guild or participate in these meetings was like committing business suicide. The pressure to participate became the chief issue which faced the members of the church. The members of the Thyatira church found themselves justifying the meeting events, which eventually allowed them to make acceptance of the events a part of their theology; causing them to disregard their participation in idolatry and fornication. As they increased financially, the members of the church tried to compensate God by giving generously, hoping He would take the matter into consideration and overlook their sin. As we continue to look into the previous Scripture reference, we find that Lydia had a strong desire to prove to Paul that she was faithful to the Lord. This may have come from the fact that many others declaring to be Christians in her city were unfaithful. Her desire to prove this to Paul caused her to make them stay with her in her home. She wanted to show them that her devotion to God was real and genuine. The Scripture says, "she constrained us". In Greek, this word "constrained" means "to employ force contrary to what is natural and right".

Another interesting thing about Thyatira is that those who made the garments of purple knew what the purple cloth represented in the society in which they lived. When a woman wore purple it presented her to the world as upright and virtuous. Most of us know of the reference given to us in Proverbs 31:10-31 of the virtuous woman.

Who can find a virtuous woman? for her price is far above rubies. The heart of her husband doth safely trust in her, so that he shall have no need of spoil. She will do him good and not evil all the days of her life. She seeketh wool, and flax, and worketh willingly with her hands. She is like the merchants' ships; she bringeth her food from afar. She riseth also while it is yet night, and giveth meat to her household, and a portion to her maidens. She considereth a field, and buyeth it: with the fruit of her hands she planteth a vineyard. She girdeth her loins with strength, and strengthened her arms. She perceiveth that her merchandise is good: her candle goeth not out by night. She layeth her hands to the spindle, and her hands hold the distaff. She stretcheth out her hand to the poor; yea, she reacheth forth her hands to the needy. She is not afraid of the snow for her household: for all her

household are clothed with scarlet. She maketh herself coverings of tapestry; her clothing is silk and purple. Her husband is known in the gates, when he sitteth among the elders of the land. She maketh fine linen, and selleth it; and delivereth girdles unto the merchant. Strength and honour are her clothing; and she shall rejoice in time to come. She openeth her mouth with wisdom; and in her tongue is the law of kindness. She looketh well to the ways of her household, and eateth not the bread of idleness. Her children arise up, and call her blessed; her husband also, and he praiseth her. Many daughters have done virtuously, but thou excellest them all. Favor is deceitful, and beauty is vain: but a woman that feareth the LORD, she shall be praised. Give her of the fruit of her hands; and let her own works praise her in the gates.

When we look at the virtuous woman, we become aware that her husband can trust her to make right decisions. It says that her husband has "no need of spoil". The word, "spoil" means, "dubious gain". A virtuous woman knows that she does not need to be involved in fornication and idolatry to bring in riches or gain. It goes on to say that a virtuous woman will do her husband good and not evil. The word for "good" here means "right in God's eyes". Any gain that is not right in the eyes of God will bring evil upon the house. You notice in this Scripture that her house is dressed in scarlet or purple and she wears silk that is purple. It is ironic to think that the Thyatira church made this material that represented virtue but prostituted themselves to the unions for money. Towards the end of this text it says, "Favor is deceitful and beauty is vain, but the fear of the Lord will cause her to be praised". The word combination "favor is deceitful" simply means "acceptance in the eyes of men will deceive and make you false". The word combination "beauty is vain" means "to make yourself look good out of a desire to promote yourself". Because money caused the church of Thyatira to refuse to stop participating in fornication and idolatry, they lost their virtue and true love for Jesus Christ. They used their wealth and success to try to impress the Lord with giving and doing great works for the Lord. By outward appearance men would think that they truly loved God.

In Revelation 2:18 it says that Jesus is coming to this church with "eyes as flaming fire and feet like fine brass". In Greek the definitions mean "his eyes are filled with burning anger and his feet are coming to step on this church as He would step on an enemy". The word "brass" is a combination of words that can imply "holy judgment in regards to money". As the text in Revelation moves forward, we hear the Lord talk about the things the church has done. We notice that they started with works and they ended with works. The word "works" means "business or that which one is occupied with". The word "works" is connected to the Greek word *ergon* which means "enterprise accomplished by hand, art, industry, or mind". Scripture tells us that when we operate in line with God's will that God will bless the work of our hands. The key to finding out the difference in the last works and the first works is revealed to us in the meaning of the portion of text, which says, "the last to be more than the first." The word "last" means "to lay hold of things or possessions to prove one's worth". The word for "more" means "to consider more valuable or greater in quality than"; the word for "first" means "the original purpose". In essence, when placed together Jesus is saying that the church of Thyatira thinks that the possession of things is more valuable to the kingdom of God than fulfilling God's original will and purpose. In their minds the possessions actually validate their worth in the eyes of God. Jesus then says that they allowed the woman Jezebel to teach them to fornicate and commit idolatry. Many people think that there was an actual prophetess in the historic church of Thyatira who validated the people's compromise by using false gifts. Whether this is true or not is not the point. The spirit behind Jezebel has always seduced people to compromise. Whether it was a woman or a man that caused the church to compromise makes no difference to the Lord. It's all Jezebel to Him. No matter how spiritual and good the concept of gain through compromise sounds, it is never permissive to God. Jesus says that He even gave this church room to repent, but she refused to do so. He then addresses her offspring or children. I believe that this represents every church and ministry who was birthed out of this teaching and doctrine. The word "offspring" means "one that depends on it, is possessed by a desire or affection toward it, or addicted to it." Across this country there are hundreds of ministers and ministries addicted to the idea of success and gain to prove that God is validating their ministry. There is a drive and affection towards the idea of big buildings, big congregations, wealth, and personal gain. Those who hold these views think that acquiring earthly possessions, attaining great followings, and building earthly kingdoms prove that they carry stronger authority and greater anointing. Jesus says that He will kill this offspring and all the churches will know that He searches the reins of the heart. This is a picture of what Jehu did to the house of Ahab in 2 Kings Chapter 10 where he destroyed everything that remained of Jezebels' seed and followers. The Lord rewards Jehu for fulfilling what was right in His eyes and fulfilling what was in His heart. The job of the true church is to please the Lord, before we please ourselves. Again, the Lord speaks to those who may be in these types of churches and ministries but have failed to adhere to this doctrine. He simply says to hold fast until He comes. Then in Revelation 2:26 we are given the key to overcome this false doctrine, ***And he that overcometh, and keepeth my works unto the end,***

to him will I give power over the nations. The word "overcometh" means "to conquer in victory." All of us must let the Lord have free reign in our lives so we can be victorious over the works of the flesh. You then notice that God gives us all a direct order to keep His works, not ours. We are to be about the Father's business, even to the end. His business is not our business, church business, or even the world's business. It's His, He owns His Church. The words "the end" simply means "the last purpose." This means that the purpose we start with has to be His and the purpose we end with has to be His. Our hearts have to be filled with the desire to please Him alone. We cannot be swayed by other loves. He will not share His devotion with another.

As we bring this chapter to a close, we need to understand that Jesus will fulfill the law even when it comes to His bride. He will not share her with another. When it comes to fornication and harlotry, even Jesus believes in divorce. Not all those who say they are His are truly His and He will be separated from any church that will not commit to Him. Deuteronomy 24:1-4 says,

When a man hath taken a wife, and married her, and it come to pass that she find no favor in his eyes, because he hath found some uncleanness in her: then let him write her a bill of divorcement, and give it in her hand, and send her out of his house. And when she is departed out of his house, she may go and be another man's wife. And if the latter husband hate her, and write her a bill of divorcement, and giveth it in her hand, and sendeth her out of his house; or if the latter husband die, which took her to be his wife; Her former husband, which sent her away, may not take her again to be his wife, after that she is defiled; for that is abomination before the LORD: and thou shalt not cause the land to sin, which the LORD thy God giveth thee for an inheritance.

After we have given ourselves over to complete harlotry and Jesus has completely separated from us, there is a point that union is not possible. When our uncleanness causes us to pursue the wrong spirit over the Holy Spirit, there is a point of no return. The bride of Christ must commit herself only to Christ. She must not toy with false doctrine or false spirits. We all need to remember Isaiah 54:5, ***For thy Maker is thine husband; the LORD of hosts is his name; and thy***

Redeemer the Holy One of Israel; The God of the whole earth shall he be called. The bride that overcomes the spirit of loving the world, money, and gain is told that she will rule the nations of the earth with power, with a rod of iron, and that she would shatter the clay pots into pieces all because of her alliance with the One true authority, Jesus Christ. In Psalms 2:8-12 we find the Lord speaking to his bride prophetically when he says,

Ask of me, and I shall give thee the heathen for thine inheritance, and the uttermost parts of the earth for thy possession. Thou shalt break them with a rod of iron; thou shalt dash them in pieces like a potter's vessel. Be wise now therefore, O ye kings: be instructed, ye judges of the earth. Serve the LORD with fear, and rejoice with trembling. Kiss the Son, lest he be angry, and ye perish from the way, when his wrath is kindled but a little. Blessed are all they that put their trust in him.

This powerful Scripture repeats the same theme given to those who will overcome the doctrine of the church of Thyatira. It is a declaration from the Father to the bride who will stand and love Jesus Christ alone. Make a decision today not to give in and yield to the things of the world and you will reap the benefits of ruling and reigning with Jesus Christ. We each have this promise if we will simply obey,

He taught me also, and said unto me, Let thine heart retain my words: keep my commandments, and live. (Proverbs 4:4)

Chapter 5

The Dead Church

And I, brethren, when I came to you, came not with excellency of speech or of wisdom, declaring unto you the testimony of God. For I determined not to know any thing among you, save Jesus Christ, and him crucified. And I was with you in weakness, and in fear, and in much trembling. And my speech and my preaching was not with enticing words of man's wisdom, but in demonstration of the Spirit and of power: That your faith should not stand in the wisdom of men, but in the power of God.

I Corinthians 2:1-5

One of the greatest fights ever waged within the world of the religious church is the fine balance between the spiritual and the logical. There are many in the church world who fails to obey the complete and inerrant Word of God because there are parts contained within its pages that seem impossible to receive. Those who want to focus on their spiritual walk with God choose to avoid Scripture that deals with the responsibility of personal action and the works of the flesh. Those who focus on logic deny the miraculous in the Word and limit the power of God by telling God what He can or cannot do. The Word of God is not only a work of the Spirit, but it is a book of law that pertains to the natural consequences of sin in the earth. The logic of man and the Spiritual works of God seem to be at war. Because this war has been waged throughout the centuries, we need to understand that the Lord designed logic and spirit to be brought together to produce balance in our lives. When God made man, He gave him abilities in both arenas. While man is a spiritual being, he also has the ability to gain knowledge and use intellect to make choices in his everyday life. Within this life you will find that individuals yield themselves to one side or the other. Those who are primarily spiritual take no responsibility for their actions and blame the condition of their life on demonic activity. Those who are logical almost deny the existence of the spirit realm and trust themselves to the point that logic becomes their god. It's time that the Church realizes that the balancing of these two sides is the place that true authority occurs. Those who yield themselves only to the spiritual side in their walk with Christ are in danger because without the Word to give direction to the things of the Spirit, you will not know what spirit you are of. On the contrary, those who trust in personal wisdom and logic become their own gods and will have to be able to set themselves free from sin without the assistance and the power of the Holy Spirit.

Now that we see the two sides of the issue, understand that denominations and church organizations tend to yield to one side or the other as well. Men establish works based on what they are comfortable with in God's Word instead of taking all of God's Word and making it the foundation. The more of God's Word we can adhere to, the more balanced and complete the work of God will be in the lives of the congregation, and in the lives of the leadership. When we pick, choose, and determine the parts of the Word of God we will believe, then we will remain unbalanced and real growth will become difficult. We need to remember that the Word of God was given to men through the work of the Holy Spirit. If the men that wrote the Scripture failed to give themselves over to the Holy Spirit, then the Word would be mere opinion and our faith would lie in the wisdom of men. In fact, our Bible was formed out of the agreement of books not the disagreements of men. Still men dissect every word and try to determine what is meant by the text. We use our own logic to determine what Scripture is for our day. In 2 Peter 1:16-2:3, Peter says,

"For we have not followed cunningly devised fables, when we made known unto you the power and coming of our Lord Jesus Christ, but were eyewitnesses of his majesty. For he received from God the Father honour and glory, when there came such a voice to him from the excellent glory, This is my beloved Son, in whom I am well pleased. And this voice which came from heaven we heard, when we were with him in the holy mount. We have also a more sure word of prophecy; whereunto ye do well that ye take heed, as unto a light that shineth in a dark place, until the day dawn, and the day star arise in

your hearts: Knowing this first, that no prophecy of the scripture is of any private interpretation. For the prophecy came not in old time by the will of man: but holy men of God spake as they were moved by the Holy Ghost. But there were false prophets also among the people, even as there shall be false teachers among you, who privily shall bring in damnable heresies, even denying the Lord that bought them, and bring upon themselves swift destruction. And many shall follow their pernicious ways; by reason of whom the way of truth shall be evil spoken of. And through covetousness shall they with feigned words make merchandise of you: whose judgment now of a long time lingereth not, and their damnation slumbereth not."

Peter starts out by saying that what he has experienced is not a fable or a story from men; it is a reality. He experienced the power of God. He then continues to say that there is no private interpretation of Scripture. It is our job to take all of the Word of God and do what it says. We need to remember that the true writer of the Scripture is the Holy Ghost. Therefore, if you hate the spiritual side of the Gospel, you then teach from your own intellect. Those who teach the Word of God from the point of logic only, or from the point of spirit only, will ultimately be teaching false doctrine. In our day, false teaching will be the major issue. Every minister, church, and organization must first give the Holy Spirit free reign so we can rightly divide the Word of truth. If the Holy Spirit gave men the words to write then He alone has the true interpretation and understanding. I believe this is why Jesus says in John 16:13,

"Howbeit when he, the Spirit of truth, is come, he will guide you into all truth: for he shall not speak of himself; but whatsoever he shall hear, that shall he speak: and he will show you things to come. He shall glorify me: for he shall receive of mine, and shall show it unto you."

If we use our logic to try to live the Word of God, the result will always be horrible failure. To deny the power of God free demonstration of the Word in our lives is to say that we can change ourselves without the assistance of the Holy Spirit. The failure of human logic to be able to make the right choice after knowing the truth is the real reason Christ came. Sin is the inability to obey what is known to be right. Through the law the Jewish people were given clear understanding between right and wrong. They were given a list of dos and don'ts, but having a logical knowledge of the law did not keep them from breaking it. James 4:17 tells us what sin is when it says, ***Therefore to him that knoweth to do good, and doeth [it] not, to him it is sin.*** It was impossible for the Jewish people to obey the law without having the power of the Holy Spirit in operation in their lives. The Holy Spirit is the Spirit of God and by right should be given to Jesus alone. God is Holy so His Spirit can only dwell in a pure vessel free from sin. Jesus paid the price for our sin and His blood covers us. Accepting Jesus Christ as our Savior and giving Him Lordship in our life frees us from sin and gives the Holy Spirit free reign to teach us the ways of God. Romans 7:4-13 gives us a powerful example about the law and sin it says,

Wherefore, my brethren, ye also are become dead to the law by the body of Christ; that ye should be married to another, even to him who is raised from the dead, that we should bring forth fruit unto God. For when we were in the flesh, the motions of sins, which were by the law, did work in our members to bring forth fruit unto death. But now we are delivered from the law, that being dead wherein we were held; that we should serve in newness of spirit, and not in the oldness of the letter. What shall we say then? Is the law sin? God forbid. Nay, I had not known sin, but by the law: for I had not known lust,

except the law had said, Thou shalt not covet. But sin, taking occasion by the commandment, wrought in me all manner of concupiscence. For without the law sin was dead. For I was alive without the law once: but when the commandment came, sin revived, and I died. And the commandment, which was ordained to life, I found to be unto death. For sin, taking occasion by the commandment, deceived me, and by it slew me. Wherefore the law is holy, and the commandment holy, and just, and good. Was then that which is good made death unto me? God forbid. But sin, that it might appear sin, working death in me by that which is good; that sin by the commandment might become exceeding sinful.

In this verse you notice a direct difference made between the old way of serving God and the new way through the work of the Holy Spirit. Here the Scripture says that we no longer need to serve God by mere logic or letter, we need to learn to serve in the newness of Spirit. Paul goes onto say that the law of God is holy and right and good, but not being able to obey the law causes death to come through sin. Another powerful Scripture that shows balance between the Spirit and the Word is found in 2 Corinthians 3:4-18.

And such trust have we through Christ to God-ward:

Not that we are sufficient of ourselves to think anything as of ourselves; but our sufficiency is of God; Who also hath made us able ministers of the new testament; not of the letter, but of the spirit: for the letter killeth, but the spirit giveth life. But if the ministration of death, written and engraven in stones, was glorious, so that the children of Israel could not steadfastly behold the face of Moses for the glory of his countenance; which glory was to be done away: How shall not the ministration of the spirit be rather glorious? For if the ministration of condemnation be glory, much more doth the ministration of righteousness exceed in glory. For even that which was made glorious had no glory in this respect, by reason of the glory that excelleth. For if that which is done away was glorious, much more that which remaineth is glorious. Seeing then that we have such hope, we use great plainness of speech: And not as Moses, which put a veil over his face, that the children of Israel could not steadfastly look to the end of that which is abolished: But their minds were blinded: for until this day remaineth the same veil untaken away in the reading of the old testament; which veil is done away in Christ. But even unto this day, when Moses is read, the veil is upon their heart. Nevertheless when it shall turn to the Lord, the veil shall be taken away. Now the Lord is that Spirit: and where the Spirit of the Lord is, there is liberty. But we all, with open face beholding as in a glass the glory of the Lord, are changed into the same image from glory to glory, even as by the Spirit of the Lord.

Those who try to obey Scripture by human logic are simply making a statement to God that says they are self-sufficient. Paul says we are able ministers of the New Testament by being of the Spirit. He then goes on to say the Word kills, but the Spirit brings life. As he continues, he makes an analogy between the work of the old and new by using a reference to Moses. He shows the old being abolished by Moses covering His face so the people would not know that He had lost the power. Basically, what he is saying is that those who deny the operation of the Holy Spirit in their lives are fooling themselves. They have no power to prove the Word they preach because it is the Holy Spirit that brings the liberty they seek. If you serve the Lord through human logic you will have to learn to live with your sin because you will fail. Denominations and organizations that teach the Word through logic only tend to also teach acceptance of sin. If we deny the power of God through the work of the Holy Spirit, we end up preaching a powerless gospel that applies grace only. Galatians 5:16-17 says,

This I say then, Walk in the Spirit, and ye shall not

fulfill the lust of the flesh. For the flesh wars against the Spirit, and the Spirit against the flesh: and these are contrary the one to the other: so that ye cannot do the things that ye would.

Jesus Christ set us free from sin so we would not have to be in bondage to it. The Holy Spirit is given to teach us to overcome sin by revealing the truth of the Word of God to us, and giving us the power and the grace to walk out what we know.

In Revelation chapter 3, we find a letter from Jesus Christ to the church of Sardis.

And unto the angel of the church in Sardis write; These things saith he that hath the seven Spirits of God, and the seven stars; I know thy works, that thou hast a name that thou livest, and art dead. Be watchful, and strengthen the things which remain, that are ready to die: for I have not found thy works perfect before God. Remember therefore how thou hast received and heard, and hold fast, and repent. If therefore thou shalt not watch, I will come on thee as a thief, and thou shalt not know what hour I will come upon thee. Thou hast a few names even in Sardis which have not defiled their garments; and they shall walk with me in white: for they are worthy. He that overcometh, the same shall be

clothed in white raiment; and I will not blot out his name out of the book of life, but I will confess his name before my Father, and before his angels. He that hath an ear, let him hear what the Spirit saith unto the churches.

Historically, the city of Sardis was one that went from extreme wealth to one of complete deterioration. The greatest moment of wealth for the city was when it was ruled by Croesus. Many reference the great wealth accumulated by this man by using the phrase "As rich as Croesus". The city developed a reputation as a powerful city of wealth and fortune. Towards the end of Croesus rule he consulted some oracles that prophesied his alliance with some other governments, which in the end would get the whole city destroyed. Maybe the greatest point to be made of the city of Sardis is that you can have a good reputation and still be destroyed by listening to false spirits and false reasoning. Jesus starts out His letter to the church of this city by making reference to the fact the He has the seven Spirits of God, and holds the seven stars of God. To many people these two statements can seem quite confusing. Revelation 1:2 reveals who the seven stars are and who the seven candlesticks are.

The mystery of the seven stars which thou sawest in my right hand, and the seven golden candlesticks. The seven stars are the angels of the seven churches: and the seven candlesticks which thou sawest are the seven churches.

So here we see that the seven stars represent the ministers who preach to the seven churches. They are in Jesus' hand and are to be controlled by Him. Every minister is set in place to preach the whole counsel of God delivered to us by Jesus Christ. We are not called to adapt, adjust, add to or take away from the Word of God. We need to remember that Jesus Christ is the very Word of God. He is not Word only; He is also full of the Spirit of God. At the beginning of this letter to Sardis it says that Jesus has the seven Spirits of God. The number seven represents perfection, completion and fullness. We all know that there is only one Holy Spirit, but the Church must desire the operation of the Holy Spirit in its fullness. We need to allow the Holy Spirit to complete His work in our lives. The fact that Jesus came to Sardis in the fullness of the Holy Spirit and in control of the ministers has to reveal to us that these things were lacking in this church. Revelation 5:8 gives us further insight to the statement seven Spirits of God.

And I beheld, and, lo, in the midst of the throne and of the four beasts, and in the midst of the elders, stood a Lamb as it had been slain, having seven horns and seven eyes, which are the seven Spirits of God sent forth into all the earth.

Here it is revealed that the Lamb had seven horns and seven eyes and these are the seven Spirits of God. When you look into the Greek words for "horns" and "eyes" you find that the word for "horns" means "a mighty valiant helper" and "eyes" means "the faculty of knowing." So the Lamb had the perfect mighty valiant helper and the perfect faculty of knowing which is the fullness or complete work of the Holy Spirit. In the Greek it does not show "Spirits" as plural. This must have happened during translation to the English language because of the number seven being in front of this word.

As we continue to look into this text we find a similar prophesy to Zerubbabel in Zechariah chapter 4. Zerubbabel was the first leader to lead the Jews out of captivity from Babylon. His name means "to dry up or to be scorched by mixing." We cannot mix our logic in with the work of the Holy Spirit. If we do, we are sure to be led into captivity. The prophesy given to Zechariah for Zerubbabel is in 4:2-6.

And said unto me, What seest thou? And I said, I have looked, and behold a candlestick all of gold, with a bowl upon the top of it, and his seven lamps thereon, and seven pipes to the seven lamps, which are upon the top thereof: And two olive trees by it, one upon the right side of the bowl, and the other upon the left side thereof. So I answered and spake to the angel that talked with me, saying, What are these, my lord? Then the angel that talked with me answered and said unto me, Knowest thou not what these be? And I said, No, my lord. Then he answered and spake unto me, saying, This is the word of the LORD unto Zerubbabel, saying, Not by might, nor by power, but by my spirit, saith the LORD of hosts.

The divine answer to keep Israel from returning to captivity is given in this prophecy. ***"Not by might, nor by power, but by my spirit, saith the Lord".*** This is the key that Israel needed to go forward in the things of

God. Not logic or more law. They lacked the ability to obey the law because they were not Spirit-led. Their inability to carry the Spirit of God is what led them to Babylon in the first place. The only way to keep from being judged is for all of us to be led completely by the Spirit of God. The prophecy continues in verses 7-14.

Who art thou, O great mountain? before Zerubbabel thou shalt become a plain: and he shall bring forth the headstone thereof with shoutings, crying, Grace, grace unto it. Moreover the word of the LORD came unto me, saying, The hands of Zerubbabel have laid the foundation of this house; his hands shall also finish it; and thou shalt know that the LORD of hosts hath sent me unto you. For who hath despised the day of small things? for they shall rejoice, and shall see the plummet in the hand of Zerubbabel with those seven; they are the eyes of the LORD, which run to and fro through the whole earth. Then answered I, and said unto him, What are these two olive trees upon the right side of the candlestick and upon the left side thereof? And I answered again, and said unto him, What be these two olive branches which through the two golden pipes empty the golden oil out of themselves? And he answered me and said, Knowest thou not what these be? And I said, No, my lord. Then said he, These are the two anointed ones, that stand by the Lord of the whole earth.

If Zerubbabel yields to the Holy Spirit the mountain will become plain, and they will bury their enemies. The Word of the Lord is that Zerubbabel and those seven will defeat the enemy. It then says that those seven are the eyes of the Lord that we have already referenced in Revelation 5:8 as being the complete or full work of the Holy Spirit. All of these points have been established to give us clarification about the church of Sardis. From the very beginning of this letter we establish that the ministers need to submit to the control of Jesus Christ, and that this church needs to focus on operating in the fullness of the Holy Spirit. The work of the Holy Spirit is not only to teach us, but in John 16:13 it says that the Holy Spirit will also tell us things to come. A few lines down in this letter to Sardis we see that Jesus tells them, ***"If therefore thou shalt not watch, I will come on thee as a thief and thou shalt not know what hour I will come upon thee."*** In Scripture we find several references to the word "watch." A few instances can be found in Mark 13:24-37 and in Matthew 24:14-24:32. The meaning of the word "watch" in Greek is "a set time to be on guard to make sure that your actions are in obedience to God's desires." It also says, "by being active one will avoid disease, death, and loss of the anointing." In the reference in Matthew, we are given the story of the ten virgins. Five of the virgins had no oil in their lamps. Because they lacked the oil, they had no fire to light their lamps and they were denied entrance into the marriage ceremony. Without the complete work of the Holy Spirit in our lives, we will be denied.

As the letter continues, Jesus continues to deal with the issue of appearances. The church of Sardis had developed the ability to appear alive, but it was dead. It had works that made people think that it was on the right track, but without the fullness of the Holy Spirit, it was failing. It needed to be strengthened by the Holy Spirit. God looked down and saw that the works that it accomplished were not perfect. Again, we can reference the number seven, which means complete, perfected, and full. Trying to do works to keep up religious appearances has always been an issue with God. Jesus Christ wants a real relationship with His Church. This relationship does not come through works; it comes through yielding to the work of the Holy Spirit. When Jesus walked on the earth this was the major area of discussion between Him and the religious leaders of His day. The religious leaders perverted the laws and the doctrines of God and used them to hold people in religious bondage. As we progress though this letter to Sardis you will see three areas that Jesus draws attention to, that we will address with Scripture. They are the fullness of the Holy Spirit, returning to the doctrine of Christ, and the ability to walk in true authority. We have already dealt with the fullness of the Holy Spirit. Now let's look at the Scripture that will address the other two issues. Let's start with the text in Matthew 7:15-29.

Beware of false prophets, which come to you in sheep's clothing, but inwardly they are ravening wolves. Ye shall know them by their fruits. Do men gather grapes of thorns, or figs of thistles? Even so every good tree bringeth forth good fruit; but a corrupt tree bringeth forth evil fruit. A good tree cannot bring forth evil fruit, neither can a corrupt tree bring forth good fruit. Every tree that bringeth not forth good fruit is hewn down, and cast into the fire. Wherefore by their fruits ye shall know them. Not every one that saith unto me, Lord, Lord, shall

enter into the kingdom of heaven; but he that doeth the will of my Father which is in heaven. Many will say to me in that day, Lord, Lord, have we not prophesied in thy name? and in thy name have cast out devils? and in thy name done many wonderful works? And then will I profess unto them, I never knew you: depart from me, ye that work iniquity. Therefore whosoever heareth these sayings of mine, and doeth them, I will liken him unto a wise man, which built his house upon a rock: And the rain descended, and the floods came, and the winds blew, and beat upon that house; and it fell not: for it was founded upon a rock. And every one that heareth these sayings of mine, and doeth them not, shall be likened unto a foolish man, which built his house upon the sand: And the rain descended, and the floods came, and the winds blew, and beat upon that house; and it fell: and great was the fall of it. And it came to pass, when Jesus had ended these sayings, the people were astonished at his doctrine: For he taught them as one having authority, and not as the scribes.

In this text the first thing Jesus addresses right out of the box is the ability of men to carry false appearances. They look like sheep outwardly, but inwardly they are wolves ready to devour those who follow them. Jesus then proceeds to tell us how to recognize those who are false. The key given to us is to look at the fruit coming forth in their lives. It is impossible to bring forth good fruit in your life without the assistance and work of the Holy Spirit. Galatians 5:22-24 says,

But the fruit of the Spirit is love, joy, peace, longsuffering, gentleness, goodness, faith, meekness, temperance: against such there is no law. And they that are Christ's have crucified the flesh with the affections and lusts. If we live in the Spirit, let us also walk in the Spirit.

Here we see that the fruit that Jesus desires in our lives is called the fruit of the Spirit. These words should tell us all that the Holy Spirit is the only One who can change us so we bring forth fruit. The work of the Holy Spirit is to help us do the will of the Father that will bring change and growth in our lives.

In Matthew chapter 7, as Jesus proceeds, He addresses not only those who are practicing law by logic; He also addresses those who use spiritual gifts without bearing forth fruit. He then gives us a story of two men who built on two different foundations. The very last line of text tells us that Jesus taught as

One having authority, and not as the scribes. To understand this statement, you have to understand that He was still referring to the foundations. Jesus taught with the authority and the power of the Holy Spirit. The scribes on the other hand taught from a logical point of view. In the Old Testament the Holy Spirit would rest at times upon three types of individuals: the priest, the prophet, and the king. Men who carried these types of anointing wrote all of the books of the Old Testament. The scribes were the individuals who made manuscripts and recorded what was spoken. The scribes were the ones who memorized the words of the law and kept up with the documents from generation to generation. After the manuscripts were written, the scribes would allow the ink to dry and then preserve the written document by placing it in a container of sand. When Jesus made the reference of foundations, He said that one was built upon a rock and the other type of foundation was built upon the sand. Jesus was speaking directly to the scribes and their logical way of interpreting the Word of God that had been written. The scribes and the Pharisees actually longed for the power that was on those who wrote the Old Testament books. Over time the Jewish people practiced law out of logic instead of trusting those who were filled with the Spirit. In fact, jealousy caused the scribes to murder those who were filled with the Spirit of God. Matthew 23:29-37 tells us what the scribes had done.

Woe unto you, scribes and Pharisees, hypocrites! because ye build the tombs of the prophets, and garnish the sepulchres of the righteous, And say, If we had been in the days of our fathers, we would not have been partakers with them in the blood of the prophets. Wherefore ye be witnesses unto yourselves, that ye are the children of them which killed the prophets. Fill ye up then the measure of your fathers. Ye serpents, ye generation of vipers, how can ye escape the damnation of hell? Wherefore, behold, I send unto you prophets, and wise men, and scribes: and some of them ye shall kill and crucify; and some of them shall ye scourge in your synagogues, and persecute them from city to city: That upon you may come all the righteous blood shed upon the earth, from the blood of righteous Abel unto the blood of Zacharias son of Barachias, whom ye slew between the temple and the altar. Verily I say unto you, All these things shall come upon this generation. O Jerusalem, Jerusalem, thou that killest the prophets, and stonest them which are sent unto thee, how often would I have gathered thy children together, even as a hen gathereth her chickens under her wings, and ye

would not!

The whole chapter of Matthew 23 was directed at the Pharisees and the scribes that practiced the words of God out of their own intellect and reasoning without the assistance of the Holy Spirit. The scribes and the Pharisees wanted to have the authority without being submissive to the Holy Spirit. Listen to what Jesus says in Matthew 23:2-10.

"The scribes and the Pharisees sit in Moses' seat: All therefore whatsoever they bid you observe, that observe and do; but do not ye after their works: for they say, and do not. For they bind heavy burdens and grievous to be borne, and lay them on men's shoulders; but they themselves will not move them with one of their fingers. But all their works they do for to be seen of men: they make broad their phylacteries, and enlarge the borders of their garments, And love the uppermost rooms at feasts, and the chief seats in the synagogues, And greetings in the markets, and to be called of men, Rabbi, Rabbi. But be not ye called Rabbi: for one is your Master, even Christ; and all ye are brethren., and call no man your father upon the earth: for one is your Father, which is in heaven. Neither be ye called masters: for one is your Master, even Christ."

Here we see a picture of religion in control of the

lives of men. Leaders and churches that interpret the Scripture to fulfill their own purposes are basically practicing religion. Jesus tells the people not to call any man on the earth master or father. Then He gives further direction. He says that the only master is Christ. I am sure this really upset the Jews when he said Christ; in Hebrew this simply means the anointed One. So in essence He was telling them that the only master is one who is mastered by the Holy Spirit. Because the scribes and the Pharisees used their logic to interpret Scripture, it became all about works. They required men to obey the law that they themselves could not obey. The church of Sardis is still trying to operate in this same type of authority. When Jesus speaks to Sardis we see a dead work that appears alive to men. We see an authority structure that longs to wear white garments of authority, but the garments are defiled.

Woe unto you, scribes and Pharisees, hypocrites! for ye make clean the outside of the cup and of the platter, but within they are full of extortion and excess. Thou blind Pharisee, cleanse first that which is within the cup and platter, that the outside of them may be clean also. Woe unto you, scribes and Pharisees, hypocrites! for ye

are like unto whited sepulchres, which indeed appear beautiful outward, but are within full of dead men's bones, and of all uncleanness. Even so ye also outwardly appear righteous unto men, but within ye are full of hypocrisy and iniquity. (Matthew 23:25-28)

It does not matter how good the church appears from the outside, if the members within the church cannot bear forth the correct fruit, it will be cut down. Across our country there are churches that are operating out of logic instead of the Spirit of God. The Holy Spirit makes people nervous because He will convict the hearts of men and demand that they bring forth change. The Holy Spirit will make His ministers as flames of fire and cause them to speak truth no matter who it offends. All through Scripture when Jesus spoke, it cut the religious leadership and followers to the quick. The religious leaders found themselves murdering the ones sent by God, thereby breaking one of the Ten Commandments that they desired to practice. Religion cannot deliver anyone. In fact, it makes the follower worse off than when they started.

Woe unto you, scribes and Pharisees, hypocrites! for ye compass sea and land to make one proselyte,

and when he is made, ye make him twofold more the child of hell than yourselves. (Matthew 23:15)

If the leadership cannot be free from corruption, how can the follower. Those who practice religion hate the work of the Holy Spirit because it is something they cannot control. It is the work of God that speaks truth in order to bring forth power to change the individual.

The work of religion wants to cause men to be subservient to a man-made creed or doctrine. It wants individuals to trust in the ideas of men instead of allowing the individual to walk in the Spirit where they will grow in the knowledge of Jesus Christ. We have taught men to serve authority figures who have no authority in operation in their own lives. Those with true authority from God will use their authority to lead by example. The leader will allow the Holy Spirit free reign to teach him to walk the Word of God out in his personal life, before he focuses on making people obey what he cannot obey. Authority has nothing to do with the type of robe you wear, as much as it has to do with being a servant to God's Word in your life. Religion uses the robes, and the suits to make men think that they are holy, but true holiness and authority comes from within. The American church has become consumed with the way things look. We want our church building to look a certain way, our pastor to drive a certain car, our congregational members to have a certain look; all in the effort that men will know we are the true followers of God. We think that success proves to the world that God is on our side. The only way to know where God is, is to become acquainted with the Holy Spirit on a personal level. If you refuse to be Spirit-led you will be deceived. Jesus through the work of the Holy Spirit confronted false religion and doctrine to its face. The sad fact is that when God sends his messenger to confront religion in our day, many church members think that the one that is sent is in the wrong. In Acts 23:1-3 it says,

And Paul, earnestly beholding the council, said, Men and brethren, I have lived in all good conscience before God until this day. And the high priest Ananias commanded them that stood by him to smite him on the mouth. Then said Paul unto him, God shall smite thee,

thou whited wall: for sittest thou to judge me after the law, and commandest me to be smitten contrary to the law?

The law of God required that those who went to judge had to listen to the party before they made judgment. Here the High Priest has Paul smitten in the mouth because He refuses to hear the truth being spoken under the power of the Holy Spirit. There are many denominations and churches who refuse to hear Scripture spoken that they disagree with. In fact, they cannot tolerate anything that is outside their realm of logical thinking. The Word of God will judge every church. We will be required to obey it alone. To not obey the complete Word is to avoid parts of Jesus Himself. Just like physical destruction came to the city of Sardis, the same will happen to those who try to live the Word by human logic.

Because, even because they have seduced my people, saying, Peace; and there was no peace; and one built up a wall, and, lo, others daubed it with untempered mortar: Say unto them which daub it with untempered mortar, that it shall fall: there shall be an overflowing shower; and ye, O great hailstones, shall fall; and a stormy wind shall rend it. Lo, when the wall is fallen, shall it not be said unto you, Where is the daubing

wherewith ye have daubed it? (Ezekiel 13:10-12)

Religious authority focuses on the outward to prove its position. Outward appearances don't impress God. Without the proper foundation, beautiful man-made organizations will fall. It does not matter that our efforts to practice the Word of God appear right in the eyes of men. If our practice is built upon any other foundation than Jesus Christ, it will fall.

As the letter to the church of Sardis proceeds, we see Jesus saying to them, ***"remember what thou hast received and heard, hold fast to it, and repent."*** This statement has to do with following man-made doctrine, instead of the whole doctrine of Christ through the teaching of the Holy Spirit. The church of Sardis finds itself following a doctrine of bondage that even the leadership cannot perform. All of our theological writings are in vain if we cannot live what the Word says. Human thought does not matter because all of us will be held to the same account when the judgment comes. When we teach God's

Word from our own thinking, it will be tainted. Men find their favorite Scripture and from that build doctrine, denomination, and people; but God requires the whole Word to be followed. Men find one Scripture to prove their point, but God requires doctrine to be built on two or three witnesses. It is not the job of men to be able to interpret all Scripture, it is our job to yield to the Holy Spirit and let Him teach us all truth. To all of us who have built our own doctrine Jeremiah 8:8-9 says,

How do ye say, We are wise, and the law of the LORD is with us? Lo, certainly in vain made he it; the pen of the scribes is in vain. The wise men are ashamed, they are dismayed and taken: lo, they have rejected the word of the LORD; and what wisdom is in them?

It is not our job to reject any of the Scripture; it is our job to follow it. There is a point that man can become perverted in his own knowledge and reject the very Spirit of God. Those who reject the Holy Spirit will find themselves following other forms of spirituality.

For thou hast trusted in thy wickedness: thou hast said, None seeth me. Thy wisdom and thy knowledge, it

hath perverted thee; and thou hast said in thine heart, I am, and none else beside me. Therefore shall evil come upon thee; thou shalt not know from whence it riseth: and mischief shall fall upon thee; thou shalt not be able to put it off: and desolation shall come upon thee suddenly, which thou shalt not know. Stand now with thine enchantments, and with the multitude of thy sorceries, wherein thou hast laboured from thy youth; if so be thou shalt be able to profit, if so be thou mayest prevail. Thou art wearied in the multitude of thy counsels. Let now the astrologers, the stargazers, the monthly prognosticators, stand up, and save thee from these things that shall come upon thee. (Isaiah 47:10-13)

When we trust in the knowledge of men to lead, guide, and direct us, we will surely be led astray. It is our job to follow Jesus Christ, believe His Word, and to be taught by the Holy Spirit. Men who are afraid of the Holy Spirit will limit us in our efforts to be Spirit-led. They will explain away Scripture that deals with the supernatural and the evidence of God's power at work in our every day lives. Who is man to determine whether God is healer or not? That is the purpose of the Scripture. Who is man to determine who gets to go to heaven or not? That is the purpose of Scripture. Luke 11:52 says,

Woe unto you, lawyers! for ye have taken away the key of knowledge: ye entered not in yourselves, and them that were entering in ye hindered.

To the believer who follows man's logic alone there are limitations in the things of God, but the believer who follows the Holy Spirit will experience the unlimited measures of God. To those who are in the church of Sardis who still believe in the divine work of the Holy Spirit, you must learn to be Spirit led and then Jesus says that you will be dressed in white raiment and your name will stay in the Lamb's book of Life.

Chapter 6

The Beloved Church

Wherefore the rather, brethren, give diligence to make your calling and election sure: for if ye do these things, ye shall never fall: For so an entrance shall be ministered unto you abundantly into the everlasting kingdom of our Lord and Saviour Jesus Christ.

2 Peter 1:10-11

Over the last chapters we see Jesus personally addressing the varied beliefs of those who are in the divine process of kingdom citizenship. Out of all seven churches only two are given entrance into the final kingdom to rule and reign with Christ. Whether we know it or not there are requirements to be a part of kingdom of God. Those who will be married to Jesus Christ will have to obey the Word of God and be full of the Spirit of God. Throughout Scripture we find a resounding theme of people being deceived by teachings and doctrines that are not the doctrine of Christ. With so many teachings and so many different opinions it seems like an overwhelming process to try to identify the real truth. In the previous chapter we identified that it is the Holy Spirit's job to lead and guide us into all truth. If we follow the leading of the Spirit and study the Word of God we can be sure that He will teach us what we need to know as we walk out this process of becoming mature in Jesus Christ. Our greatest obstacle lies not in the search for the truth, but in our ability to remain teachable. As we grow spiritually the Holy Spirit will lead us into the deeper things of God as we continue to have a true relationship with Jesus Christ. If we determine to let denomination, religion, or individual feeling determine how far we will go with God then we are destined to fail. The practice of religion and denominationalism within the church has come at a great cost. Instead of unity and agreement being produced between the different denominations and various congregations, men have caused division by using their leadership positions to determine what is right for their congregation. In reality, the leadership in the church has manipulated the Word of God to make doctrines that suite their individual and congregational level of comfort. It is a sad day when the church has become comfortable with sin and uncomfortable with the truth of God's Word and the operation of the Holy Spirit. In our day conviction is considered offensive, and the truth of the Word is considered hate speech. Instead of making sure the people become citizens in the kingdom of God we let the offering plate determine what will be preached. Instead of encouraging men and women to develop a real relationship with Jesus Christ through the work of the Holy Spirit, leaders use church doctrine to place limits on members who are growing, and constrain the Holy Spirit so those who don't want to grow will remain comfortable and continue to give. This is the denominal pattern and apparently it is quite successful, but those who have a true experience with God have an insatiable hunger and will not be limited in their pursuit of truth. When the denomination or the congregation becomes uncomfortable with

Scripture you quote, the experience you have, or the development of Spiritual gifts then you will be kindly asked to leave. If Scripture can be found to back up the experience or the gift then the denomination or the congregations who take a stand against it stand against God.

Most denominations and congregations limit the Word of God by strictly obeying the parts that they understand. Whatever their experience has been with God is where the line is drawn doctrinally. When we focus on only the areas of the Word we are comfortable with then we become unbalanced and self-serving. Jesus Christ is the Word and to reject parts of it is to reject Him. We have denominations and church groups that basically have tunnel vision and focus only on certain areas of the Word. These areas range from salvation, water baptism, faith, prosperity, all the way to moves of God focused on a single spiritual manifestation. In heaven there will be no denomination, we are to become like Jesus Christ. Therefore, we must obey all of the Scripture in its entirety. Some of you reading this right now are overwhelmed at this statement. You are probably thinking that I want you to be like Jesus. If that is your thought process then you would be right. Too many believers think that this is impossibility. Before you blow a fuse let me take you to Matthew 22:36-40 to show you where I am going with this.

Master, which is the great commandment in the law? Jesus said unto him, Thou shalt love the Lord thy God with all thy heart, and with all thy soul, and with all thy mind. This is the first and great commandment. And the second is like unto it, Thou shalt love thy neighbor as thyself. On these two commandments hang all the law and the prophets.

Out of all the Scripture revealed to us in God's Word, Jesus places the greatest emphasis on these two commandments. The first commandment requires every believer to take away all limits concerning our love for God. Many believers limit their love for God to their hearts, but Jesus said that we have to love God with our minds, and our souls. To truly love God is not only a heart-felt experience; it has to become an experience in every area of our lives. In our minds we have to think about what

God's desires are before we serve self. The word "soul" in Greek means "life" or it can mean "mind, will, and emotions." You cannot limit your love for God to your heart; you will be required to love Him emotionally as well. You are also required to give your will over to God in your everyday life. You cannot fulfill the second great commandment until you fulfill the first. Until you love Jesus Christ in every area, you will never be able to love your brother the way you should. When you love God with everything, you will also love your brother to the point that you will not disqualify his walk with God. The last line of this text is extremely powerful. Jesus says that if you fulfill these two commandments, you will be able to fulfill all of the law and the prophets. In the Greek, the word "law" is defined as "a rule producing a state of approval by God." It is also defined as "the moral instruction given by Jesus Christ." The Greek word for "prophets" is defined as "men filled with the Spirit of God moved to speak." In essence, Jesus is saying that by obeying these two commandments you will automatically be obeying all of the Scripture, and you will also be able to speak by the Spirit. In Mark 12:29-

34, we find the same account with some additional statements.

And Jesus answered him, The first of all the commandments is, Hear, O Israel; The Lord our God is one Lord: And thou shalt love the Lord thy God with all thy heart, and with all thy soul, and with all thy mind, and with all thy strength: this is the first commandment. And the second is like, namely this, Thou shalt love thy neighbor as thyself. There is no other commandment greater than these. And the scribe said unto him, Well, Master, thou hast said the truth: for there is one God; and there is none other but he: And to love him with all the heart, and with all the understanding, and with all the soul, and with all the strength, and to love his neighbor as himself, is more than all whole burnt offerings and sacrifices. And when Jesus saw that he answered discreetly, he said unto him, Thou art not far from the kingdom of God. And no man after that durst ask him any question.

In addition to the heart, mind, and soul, Mark adds the word "strength." This reference to "strength" takes it to the point of even loving the Lord your God with your physical body and ability. In this text reference from Mark, after the scribe hears these things he responds to the Lord by agreeing with Him. Jesus then gives a powerful response; he tells the scribe ***"thou art not far from the kingdom of God."*** To obtain citizenship into the kingdom of God we have to maintain our relationship with God by focusing on fulfilling these two commandments. These two commandments require the same thing of all of us. First, we are to love God in every area of our being. Second, we are to love our brother just like we love ourselves. The lack of unity between the various denominations, ministries, and churches comes from failure to obey these commandments. Self-serving leadership and controlling congregations are made by refusing to obey these two commandments. False doctrine and every evil work come from our failure to obey these two commandments. Galatians 5:13-15 says,

For, brethren, ye have been called unto liberty; only use not liberty for an occasion to the flesh, but by love serve one another. For all the law is fulfilled in one word, even in this; Thou shalt love thy neighbor as thyself. But if ye bite and devour one another, take heed that ye be not consumed one of another.

If we love God with all of our being, then we will not make room for the comfort of our flesh. By loving God's Word and the work of the Holy Spirit we will be able to love our brother above our own doctrinal issues. In reality, most of us just love Jesus in our hearts. Because we refuse Jesus entrance into the other areas of our lives it gives room for the works of the flesh. We allow our personal feelings and opinions to place limits on someone else's experience with God. If you truly love your brother, you should want him to get as close to Jesus Christ as possible.

Separations within the various Christian denominations and entities remain because man has a predisposition to a certain sin called pride. The idea that any one group has the perfect interpretation of God's Word is ludicrous. Every group loves to prove their point by focusing on specific verses to validate their cause. The problem with this is that we will have to give an answer for all the Scripture we refuse to accept because it goes against our point of view. As believers and followers of Jesus Christ we will answer for the parts of God's Word that we reject. The safest way to find sound doctrine is to find two or three Scriptures that bring clarity to a subject by referencing the topic at hand. Anyone can find a single

Scripture reference and twist it to say what they want it to say. It becomes much more difficult when you try to find two or three. As you search Scripture, you will find that every line appropriately applied will bring clarity to the issue or topic at hand. Once truth is obtained, Scripture then only becomes powerful when it is applied and activated in your everyday life. After all is said and done, the greatest teacher will always be the Holy Spirit Himself. He will use the Scripture to bring actual growth as we submit to His leading. The Holy Spirit will be able to deal with the most prevalent need in your life just at the right time. Making doctrine an issue of personal pride to argue defeats the original intent of Scripture and makes us practice religion instead of relationship. The Scripture is not something just to debate over, it is Jesus made alive in our everyday lives. It is our job to love every line of the Word of God. It is also our job to love our brother as the Lord reveals the Word to him as well. Our knowledge is not to be used to make our brother conform to our wisdom. Every Christian has a personal responsibility to God to get wisdom by studying the Word. As we love God, we will find that the Holy Spirit will assist us in our efforts to rightly divide the Word of truth. Those who fail to continue to grow in the things of God will end up practicing a form of godliness without power to perform the Word they have received.

As we walk with God there is place where we can become so arrogant in our knowledge that we don't know what we think we know. Many times, the Holy Spirit is trying to teach us something new, but we fail to receive it because we make a form out of yesterday's knowledge. What I need to learn today will probably be different than what I learned years ago. We can become so sure in our knowing that we fail to hear what God has taught our brother. We find ourselves using our spiritual knowledge to disqualify the experience of others within the Church. It is one thing if the experience is not in line with the Word; it is another if we hinder our brother or make him conform to our experience. Most of the time our experiences in God have been limited to holding to the doctrine taught to us by men who we think have had an experience. Religion is simply the process of people patterning their walk with God after a certain man's or organization's experience. The only person we are to pattern our lives after is our Lord and Savior, Jesus Christ. All of us must continue to evaluate what we think we know.

Knowledge puffeth up, but charity edifieth. And if any man think that he knoweth any thing, he knoweth nothing yet as he ought to know. But if any man love God, the same is known of him. (I Corinthians 8:1)

There is a fine line that has to be drawn between our religious knowledge and love for our brother. The only thing that can bring balance to religious pride is charity itself. In this Scripture, the word "knowledge" simply means, "what man seems to be aware of." The words for "puffeth up" can be defined as "increases the natural man." The problem with religious doctrine and knowledge is that when knowledge is used to prove our point it causes the natural man to swell with pride. We hold our chests out and start a war to prove we are right. The primary goal of every believer should be to decrease the natural man and yield to the work of the Holy Spirit. This verse continues to tell us that charity or love for your brother edifies. The word "edifies" means "to build up or to cover a house like a roof." True love for your brother would cause you to build him up not tear him down. This Scripture goes on to say that when a man thinks he knows anything he knows nothing, because while we are so busy knowing we are not listening and miss what we need to know. The only thing that our brothers in Christ should walk away with after being in a discussion with us is a knowing that we really love God. Most doctrinal discussions usually end up with brotherly separation and emotional anxiety. I believe that this comes from our personal inability to believe that our brother's experience with God is genuine and real. The truth is that what we know about God is based on our personal walk with Him. Is it possible that God could manifest Himself differently to our brother? We hold onto our personal experience and doctrine and refuse to change because if we admit that there is more to God than our limited experience, then we are admitting that God might require us to experience more of Him. The key to our entire discussion should simply be where it is in Scripture. I believe that this is why the Apostle Paul made this statement in 1 Corinthians 2:2, "***For I determined not to know any thing among you, save Jesus Christ, and him crucified."*** When we are quick to come against our brother's personal walk with God then we have made ourselves judge and jury. Most of the time in religious circles we prejudge another man's experience with knowledge learned from a denomination or organization. Many times those who are arguing doctrine as fact have little or no personal experience with God at all. Before you become an expert at religion it might be wise to communicate with God first. In 1 Corinthians 4, the Corinthian people were becoming divided by following the different teachings of the various ministers who came to bring them the good news. Division came to the church by the people choosing their favorite minister and following his doctrine alone. Paul writes in verses 1-6,

Let a man so account of us, as of the ministers of Christ, and stewards of the mysteries of God. Moreover it is required in stewards, that a man be found faithful. But with me it is a very small thing that I should be judged of you, or of man's judgment: yea, I judge not mine own self. For I know nothing by myself; yet am I not hereby

justified: but he that judgeth me is the Lord. Therefore judge nothing before the time, until the Lord come, who both will bring to light the hidden things of darkness, and will make manifest the counsels of the hearts: and then shall every man have praise of God. And these things, brethren, I have in a figure transferred to myself and to Apollos for your sakes; that ye might learn in us not to think of men above that which is written, that no one of you be puffed up for one against another.

It is not our job to be all knowing. It is our job to take what we do know and apply it in our lives. Each of us will stand before the Lord and be judged by our personal faithfulness and the condition of our hearts. We should not place stock in the men who teach us, but we should place our confidence in the written Word of God. If we make denomination, ministry, or teacher more important than discovering the truth in God's Word ourselves then we will remain divided.

In the King James Version of the Bible we find the word charity used 26 times. The Scripture we referenced earlier in 1 Corinthians 8 made use of this word. Many of the newer translations have replaced the word charity with love. In the King James the

Greek word "agape" is translated "love" 87 times and "charity" 26 times. Many scholars and translators have failed to see why the King James translators would do this. In every account where the word charity is used, it is always used in relation to those in Christ loving each other. I believe the translators chose this word to make distinction between the feeling of love, love of spiritual things, our personal love for God, and the required love for fellow believers. The word charity was used to make us aware that we need to judge ourselves when dealing with issues or differences that exist with our brethren. The Webster's 1913 dictionary defines charity as "liberality in judging of men and their actions; a disposition which inclines men to put the best construction on the words and actions of others." A synonym for the word "charity" is also the word "mercy." In our current day charity is known more in the sense of money being given to those in need. When it comes to your Christian brother and his experiences in his walk with Jesus Christ, we are required to give something. We must give up our religious pride in the area of knowing everything about the things of God. If I were to define charity I would give it this definition: a disposition within a Christian which qualifies his own character in regards to actual and active relations with those of like faith. I believe that charity is the qualifying characteristic to have fruitful relationships with people within the body of Christ. Our level of maturity in Christ is revealed when we respond correctly towards those we disagree with. Too many of us cut off relationships that will require us to grow and mature. Our problem is that we think that the people in our lives are the problem. Did you ever think that God allowed you to have disagreements with people so that you would be able to develop your fruit? Most of us run from the people who are not in 100% agreement with us. Every relationship sent into your life is for a reason. The real issue is whether or not you have enough of the fruit of the Spirit to handle it. Colossians 3:12-17 says,

Put on therefore, as the elect of God, holy and beloved, bowels of mercies, kindness, humbleness of mind, meekness, longsuffering; Forbearing one another, and forgiving one another, if any man have a quarrel against any: even as Christ forgave you, so also do ye. And above all these things put on charity, which is the

bond of perfectness. And let the peace of God rule in your hearts, to the which also ye are called in one body; and be ye thankful. Let the word of Christ dwell in you richly in all wisdom; teaching and admonishing one another in psalms and hymns and spiritual songs, singing with grace in your hearts to the Lord. And whatsoever ye do in word or deed, do all in the name of the Lord Jesus, giving thanks to God and the Father by him.

To grow in God is to be able to carry yourself in the right way when in relationship with your brother or sister. When dealing with others in Christ we are to be merciful, kind, humble in what we think, continuing in relationship with our brother and sister in Christ for the long haul. All of these characteristics reveal the true meaning of the word "charity." Scripture clearly says that charity is the bond that leads to being perfect. Most of us hear this word perfect and feel condemned or belittled because of the ongoing imperfections in our lives. In Greek the root of the word "perfect" is *telos*. As you look into its definition you find that it means "a place of growth where one reaches a state of moral and spiritual completion." It can also mean "maturity" or even "the place that something is finished and ceases to be." We will never die to self until we make charity for our brother a focus in our walk with Christ. In order to keep good relationships with the people in the body of Christ we cannot take off our love shackle. When you operate out of love you don't say everything you think, believe everything you hear about a person from others, but you value the person God has sent for you to have relationship with. We all know that true relationship can only happen when two people yield to one another. One of the greatest problems within the Church of our day seems to be a lack of true relationship. At times our relationships with others tend to be one-sided. The side that tends to prevail is usually "my side." Scripture teaches us to value the other person more than our own self-serving motives. In fact, the only way you can become mature in Christ is to make this your practice.

The true test of brotherly love within the church is not during times of food, fun, and fellowship; it tends to be in doctrinal discussions or moments where people begin to function within the church. One of the greatest areas of contention within the body of Christ remains to be in the area of Spiritual gifts. Some churches and denominations even go as far as to say that certain gifts are demonic. I have yet to find a passage of Scripture that tells the church not to allow Spiritual gifts. Those who take this direction and mindset in the church need to find two or three Scriptures to validate their claim. If the Apostle Paul were alive today he would be rejected by the majority of denominational churches because he says in 1 Corinthians 14:18, ***"I thank my God, I speak with tongues more than ye all"***, yet he wrote a majority of the New Testament. There have been many believers asked to leave denomination or congregation simply because someone in the church found out that they received the Holy Spirit. In the churches where gifts are allowed, the gifted tend to use their gifts to take a place of spiritual authority within the church. When this happens, people begin to worship the gifted more that the gift-giver. The problem is that gifts and callings of God are without repentance. This means that the gifted person can use his gift and still suffer in his Christian walk when it comes to relationship with Jesus Christ, and relationships with others. By now you should know that I am going to take us to the love chapter in Corinthians. Many mainline denominations use these verses to try to prove that gifts were done away with, but I want us to take a good common sense look into what is really being said. To understand I Corinthians 13 you first must read and examine chapter 12. Paul starts out by talking about the diversity of gifts within the body of Christ. He says that the manifestations of the Spirit are given to profit withal. The word for "manifestations" simply means "visible or to realize." The Greek words for "profit withal" mean "to bear, bring together, to contribute or to help." The gifts of God are visual works of the Holy Spirit that bring the body of Christ together in order to help. As Paul continues to talk about Spiritual gifts he goes into the necessity of the body. He tells us that the eye needs the hand and the hand needs the eye. He says that the various body parts cannot say to any part of the body "I don't need you." The amazing thing is that there are churches all across our country saying they don't need the gifts of the Spirit. By saying such a thing they are saying they don't need these types of people in their churches. Towards the end of chapter 12, he then lists the gifts and callings of God and asks if everyone has the same gifts. When we are asked these questions, we all respond by saying "no." Let's look at the last line of text in 1 Corinthians 12:31 it reads, ***But covet earnestly the best gifts: and yet shew I unto you a more excellent way.*** Many of the mainline denominations want to quote I Corinthians 13:10 and say that the gifts ceased when Jesus came to earth. The problem is that Paul tells the Corinthians to have earnest desire or great zeal for the best spiritual gifts. Common sense tells as that Paul would not tell the Corinthians to desire something they could not have. He then goes on to say ***"and yet I shew unto you a more excellent way".*** What is this more excellent way? I believe he is saying I am going to show you a better way of using your gifts. In Greek the words for "excellent way" mean "a course of conduct without measure." Paul says I am going to show you a way to use your spiritual gifts where it will make them the most effective. Then he goes into 1 Corinthians 13.

Though I speak with the tongues of men and of

angels, and have not charity, I am become as sounding brass, or a tinkling cymbal. And though I have the gift of prophecy, and understand all mysteries, and all knowledge; and though I have all faith, so that I could remove mountains, and have not charity, I am nothing. And though I bestow all my goods to feed the poor, and though I give my body to be burned, and have not charity, it profiteth me nothing. Charity suffereth long, and is kind; charity envieth not; charity vaunteth not itself, is not puffed up, Doth not behave itself unseemly, seeketh not her own, is not easily provoked, thinketh no evil; rejoiceth not in iniquity, but rejoiceth in the truth; beareth all things, believeth all things, hopeth all things, endureth all things. Charity never faileth: but whether there be prophecies, they shall fail; whether there be tongues, they shall cease; whether there be knowledge, it shall vanish away. For we know in part, and we prophesy in part. But when that which is perfect is come, then that which is in part shall be done away. When I was a child, I spake as a child, I understood as a child, I thought as a child: but when I became a man, I put away childish things. For now we see through a glass, darkly; but then face to face: now I know in part; but then shall I know even as also I am known. And now abideth faith, hope, charity, these three; but the greatest of these is charity.

Paul immediately comes out of the box and starts listing the gifts that are available to the body. He starts by saying though I speak with the tongues of men and the tongues of angels, without brotherly love I am just making noise. Most people focus on the tongues of angels, but he also included preaching when he said the tongues of men. He then goes on to list a person who has multiple gifts. He says even if I have the gift of prophecy, all mysteries, all knowledge, and mountain moving faith, if I don't have brotherly love I am nothing. If I give everything I own to the poor, or even give my body to be burned, without love for my brother I am nothing. You see Paul not only speaks of spiritual gifts, he speaks of men doing any work for Christ without love for their brothers. Every gift given by God is simply to be used to show sincere love for your brother. Paul uses the word "I" seven times within three verses. The point is that anything you do in the context of self-promotion or pride is worthless to God. All of the gifts are for your brothers' edification. In fact every believer should prefer his brothers' gifts to his own. The Lord gives spiritual gifts and calling. Every man has been given gifts by God and has to learn to use them. The painter has to practice his gift in order to produce a painting. The pianist has to practice the gift before pleasure can come to the hearer. It is no different with those in the body of Christ desiring to use their spiritual gifts. The gift cannot be perfected until first it is put into use. For some reason the church thinks that gifted people should be perfect every time they use their gifts. I'm sorry to say that without practicing, the gift cannot be perfected. No preacher starts out preaching great sermons that move the masses; it is the continued obedience that develops the gift. How can our brothers and sisters in Christ grow in obedience to God when we forbid them to use what God has given them. If your brother is not allowed to be obedient to obey the Lord, he will be limited in his spiritual growth.

As Paul continues to speak in the context of Spiritual gifting, he then tells us what brotherly love really is. I will now go through the meanings of the words listed to describe true charity or love for your brother and his gifts. Charity patiently endures suffering, shows oneself useful, is not jealous of others, doesn't brag on itself, does not increase the natural man, doesn't act ugly, wants God's way, is not swift to anger, thinks no harm or injury, doesn't cheer on peoples character flaws, rejoices in the truth, covers in silent anticipation, puts trust in and believes in people, expects good, and continues to be a support. As you review the qualities of charity you see that it requires us all to go the extra mile. When it comes to our brother and the gifts God has given him we have to be careful to place our thoughts, opinions, and actions through the greatest gift of charity. Charity is to be demonstrated by those who will use their gifts and by those who receive from the gift of their brother. This two-way street of giving and receiving is the process that will cause those in Christ to come to maturity. Within the meanings of charity demonstrated to us in these verses in Corinthians we find that there are moments we are to suffer with our brothers and still remain in support by believing in people and expecting good. We also show charity by not bragging on ourselves, acting ugly or seeking our own way. Charity is learning to yield to others instead of yielding to self. When it comes to using our gifts, the only way for them not to fail is through charity.

The next portion of text is the Scripture reference used to try to do away with the gifts. It says that prophecies will fail, tongues will cease, and knowledge will vanish away. It goes on to say that we as people know in part, and prophesy in part. It continues by saying when that which is perfect is come that which is in part shall be done away. The reason many of the gifts of the Spirit fail is simply because they are used many times out of the influence of building up self, instead of out of God's motive of brotherly love. I have heard many preachers say "that which is perfect" is a reference to Jesus coming to earth. If the denomination wants to do away with gifts then they reference the first coming of Jesus Christ. If they like the gifts then they reference the second. Earlier we said that charity will lead us to a point of maturity or perfection in Christ. If we view this verse in this context then Paul is saying, that when all the gifts are used out of the intent of brotherly love then people will not miss the mark. In fact those using their gifting will become more accurate. This would mean that we would be mature and have the full measure of knowledge and prophecy God intended, and the church would finally grow up and put away childish thinking. It is childish to think that you know everything. It is also selfish to want things your way. The greatest gift given to the Church is the ability to prefer our brother above ourselves. If the Apostle Paul was telling us that Jesus Christ was doing away with the gifts then why does he continue in I Corinthians 14:1 by saying, ***"Follow after charity, and desire spiritual gifts".*** Common sense tells us that he was not against the use of gifting in the Church; he was against the use of gifts without the true intent of brotherly love.

Our lack of love for our brother not only restricts the operations of the gifts of the Spirit, but it also causes us to operate out of the spirit of fear. The real reason we fail to trust our brother in the area of gifts is simply because we are unable to see the motivation behind the gift. This factor of the unknown causes us to place restrictions on people to save others from being hurt. This idea of restricting gifts to preserve others is not viewed in an accurate way. Church leadership, denominations, and boards tend to operate with this mentality. They are so afraid of things getting out of hand that they are willing to stop the gifts of the Spirit in order to preserve the congregation. This is an inaccurate view and raises the question, "Who is protecting the congregation from the pastor, the board, or the leaders who all tend to have issues themselves yet expect us to continue to make room for their gifting?" Just because a pastor is an excellent preacher does not mean that he is serving out of right motive. The board members can all be serving in the church out of a desire to control the church finances, instead of out of love for their brother. I believe that this is why we are to "know those who labor among us". If Jesus had operated out of this type of mindset He would have never picked the twelve that worked for Him. The greatest way to break the mentality of fear is to hand Judas the moneybag.

If we operate out of true brotherly love we never have to worry about protecting ourselves from our enemies. Perfect love is simply trusting God to judge those with false motives while you continue to give your brothers every opportunity to do what is right by doing right yourself. All control issues within the Church are really based in the spirit of fear. The spirit of fear loves to keep us worked up over the unknown. In I Corinthians 13:12 it says, ***For now we see through a glass, darkly; but then face to face: now I know in part; but then shall I know even as also I am known.*** True brotherly love will cause all of us to mature to the point that people will be able to know us as we know ourselves. It's easy to know our own motivations. That's why we trust ourselves more than we trust others. There is a place in love that will cause you to yield your self-serving agenda and learn to trust others, so that others will know you, like you know yourself. Our ability to know others comes through the process of time and relationship. It is the process of seeing someone do the right thing over and over again that brings stability to our hearts concerning their motivation. Fear stops this process before it starts. It never lets true relationship develop because of what "might" happen. In this area of relationship with our brother we all have to learn to take risks. What we must realize is that we are just as risky as the brother we fear. Jesus took a risk on all of us when He called us to have relationship with Him. The amazing thing about God is that He already knows the outcome and still reaches out. If Jesus took the viewpoint of most of the churches, denominations, and leaders, He would have never even tried to save any of us out of fear that we would betray Him.

And we have seen and do testify that the Father sent the Son to be the Savior of the world. Whosoever shall confess that Jesus is the Son of God, God dwelleth in him, and he in God. And we have known and believed the love that God hath to us. God is love; and he that dwelleth in love dwelleth in God, and God in him. Herein is our love made perfect, that we may have boldness in the day of judgment: because as he is, so are we in this world. There is no fear in love; but perfect love casteth out fear: because fear hath torment. He that feareth is not made perfect in love. We love him, because he first loved us. If a man say, I love God, and hateth his brother, he is a liar: for he that loveth not his brother whom he hath seen, how can he love God whom he hath not seen? And this commandment have we from him, That he who loveth God love his brother also (I John 4:14-21).

The love that Jesus showed to us is not a self-serving love that loves only when things turn out well, but it is a love that stands for eternity. It stands through the possibility of mistakes and pain. It is a love that is willing to take the risk and cast out the spirit of fear that desires to break relationship. Jesus is not fearful and we are not to be fearful in the world. Perfect love casts out fear, and it refuses to control people. It continues to give opportunities to others even when there is risk involved. You cannot become mature or perfected in love when you continue to operate and make decisions out of fear. We cannot control our brothers and we cannot control the Word of God to fit our agenda. Charity is the process of our own walk to maturity in God. This walk of brotherly love not only requires us to take risks, it requires us to cover our brothers when mistakes are made. Read I Peter 4:7-11.

But the end of all things is at hand: be ye therefore sober, and watch unto prayer. And above all things have fervent charity among yourselves: for charity shall cover the multitude of sins. Use hospitality one to another without grudging. As every man hath received the gift, even so minister the same one to another, as

good stewards of the manifold grace of God. If any man speak, let him speak as the oracles of God; if any man minister, let him do it as of the ability which God giveth: that God in all things may be glorified through Jesus Christ, to whom be praise and dominion forever and ever. Amen.

The idea of fervent charity is one that stretches itself as far as possible. The word for "fervent" means "stretched out". We cannot be true believers if we give up on someone the moment they make a mistake. True charity goes the distance; it does everything in its power to look at the good in the life of its brother. True charity covers people even in their moments of missing the mark. Again, we see this Scripture deals with gifts and how we use them. All of us have a responsibility to be moved out of brotherly love and not out of self or self-preservation. We have to go beyond our fears and move out in faith so that God will be able to finish His complete work in all of our lives. It's time for the Church to turn away from false mindsets and get back to sincere love for others. I Timothy 1:5-7 reads,

Now the end of the commandment is charity out of a pure heart, and of a good conscience, and of faith

unfeigned: From which some having swerved have turned aside unto vain jangling; desiring to be teachers of the law; understanding neither what they say, nor whereof they affirm.

The end of all the commandments we follow comes back to sincere brotherly love from the heart. If we make our primary concern our brother, we will find that our personal walk increases in the knowledge of God. When we use our knowledge to try to control or manipulate to bring about our personal agenda then we are failing in the Gospel of Jesus Christ. It is possible to place too much confidence in ourselves and end up missing the mark all together. We need to value others before we value ourselves. We need to listen to others before we listen to ourselves. We need each other to walk out our walk of maturity in Jesus Christ.

In Revelation 3, we find a letter written to the church of Philadelphia. Out of all seven churches this is the only church that is given no reproof or correction. Earlier in this chapter, I told you how those who keep the two great commandments fulfill all of the law. The Greek word "Philadelphia" means "brotherly love". By fulfilling the two commandments it fulfills all of the law. If you fulfill all the law then there is nothing to correct. Revelation 3:7-13 says,

And to the angel of the church in Philadelphia write; These things saith he that is holy, he that is true, he that hath the key of David, he that openeth, and no man shutteth; and shutteth, and no man openeth; I know thy works: behold, I have set before thee an open door, and no man can shut it: for thou hast a little strength, and hast kept my word, and hast not denied my name. Behold, I will make them of the synagogue of Satan, which say they are Jews, and are not, but do lie; behold, I will make them to come and worship before thy feet, and to know that I have loved thee. Because thou hast kept the word of my patience, I also will keep thee from the hour of temptation, which shall come upon all the world, to try them that dwell upon the earth. Behold, I come quickly: hold that fast which thou hast, that no man take thy crown. Him that overcometh will I make a pillar in the temple of my God, and he shall go no more out: and I will write upon him the name of my God, and the name of the city of my God, which is new Jerusalem, which cometh down out of heaven from my God: and I will write upon him my new name. He that hath an ear, let him hear what the Spirit saith unto the churches.

Historically, the church of Philadelphia has never died. It has existed throughout time. It survived Turkish rule and today the city of Philadelphia is called "Alasehir", which means "city of God." Over the years the city went from being named the city of brotherly love to the city of God. In a sense, there is prophetic meaning behind this progression. In Jesus' final statements to the church of Philadelphia, He says that He will write on them the name of the city of God and that name would be New Jerusalem. In Revelation Chapter 21, Scripture is clear about who this New Jerusalem is and who she will be made up of.

And I John saw the holy city, new Jerusalem, coming down from God out of heaven, prepared as a bride adorned for her husband. And I heard a great voice out of heaven saying, Behold, the tabernacle of God is with men, and he will dwell with them, and they shall be his people, and God himself shall be with them, and be their God. And God shall wipe away all tears from their eyes; and there shall be no more death, neither sorrow, nor crying, neither shall there be any more pain: for the former things are passed away. And he that sat upon the throne said, Behold, I make all things new. And he said unto me, Write: for these words are true and faithful. And he said unto me, It is done. I am Alpha and

Omega, the beginning and the end. I will give unto him that is athirst of the fountain of the water of life freely. He that overcometh shall inherit all things; and I will be his God, and he shall be my son. But the fearful, and unbelieving, and the abominable, and murderers, and whoremongers, and sorcerers, and idolaters, and all liars, shall have their part in the lake which burneth with fire and brimstone: which is the second death. And there came unto me one of the seven angels which had the seven vials full of the seven last plagues, and talked with me, saying, Come hither, I will show thee the bride, the Lamb's wife. And he carried me away in the spirit to a great and high mountain, and showed me that great city, the holy Jerusalem, descending out of heaven from God (Revelation 21:2-10).

There is a city in which Jesus Christ will dwell. This city is revealed to us in this text as the bride of Christ. The bride of Christ is revealed to us as a multitude of people who have a sincere passion for Jesus. As we can clearly see from Scripture, the church of Philadelphia is the group that becomes the city of God who is the bride of Christ. In the first few lines of text we see that this bride is referenced as the holy city. In the Greek we find that the meanings behind these words are very significant. The Greek word translated "holy" is *hagios,* which not only references "holiness," but "those who are the saints of God". Many people think they qualify to be saints simply by saying the sinner's prayer or by making a one time public profession of faith. When Scripture speaks of "saints", it speaks of those who "cut off the works of sin in order to be sanctified." The sinner's prayer is the beginning of our walk with Christ that leads us to a proven place of maturity. The Greek word for "city" is *polis* which is formed from two Greek words. One is *polemos* which means "to fight a battle or to wage a war." And the other is *polys* which means "large in number." So in essence the holy city gives us a picture of a large group of sanctified people who have come to wage war. Jesus will choose a certain type of people to be the true bride of Christ. He will choose those who through the work of the Holy Spirit and the truth of the Word of God have learned to overcome sin. Only those who overcome, shall inherit all things. Only those who obey the Word, will rule and reign with Jesus Christ.

As the text continues, we are then given a list of who will not be a part of the New Jerusalem or bride of Christ. The very first group that fails to qualify are those who are fearful. Earlier we said that perfect love casts out all fear. Fear is a characteristic that opens the door to insecurity, pride, and sin. That is why the church of brotherly love is chosen to be the perfected bride. While we realize that Jesus died personally for us, we also need to recognize the heart of Jesus is not just to redeem us, but also to redeem our brothers. Jesus cannot marry a bride who will not assist Him in fulfilling His purposes. The bride of Christ has to learn to move with His heart in order to be a part of the final work. Not only are the fearful disqualified, but many others are as well. The list proceeds with the unbelieving, abominable, murderers, whoremongers, sorcerers, idolaters, and the liars. All of these will have their part in the lake of fire. The church of Philadelphia loves Jesus and their brothers enough to change. This group is not a group of intermingled sinners proclaiming to be Christian. It is a group that grows and matures in their walk with Jesus Christ and is accepted as His bride. The bride of Christ will be built upon the doctrines and the teachings of Jesus Christ. Jesus Himself through the work of the Holy Spirit will build a city called the New Jerusalem. The bride of Christ is this city. It is the building of God Himself. Scripture verifies this fact in I Corinthians 3:9 when it says, ***For we are laborers together with God: ye are God's husbandry, God's building.*** Revelation 21:14 gives further insight when it says, ***And the wall of the city had twelve foundations, and in them the names of the twelve apostles of the Lamb.*** The Apostles through the work of the Holy Spirit wrote the Scriptures of the New Testament and the foundations of New Jerusalem are based on the writings of the Apostles. Ephesians 2:19-20 agrees with this when it says,

Now therefore ye are no more strangers and foreigners, but fellow citizens with the saints, and of the household of God; And are built upon the foundation of the apostles and prophets, Jesus Christ himself being the chief corner.

This mighty bride will be made one with Jesus Christ and return to earth to establish the kingdom of God on the earth forever. She will be founded and based on the total Word of God, mature, and full of the light of God, and ready to reign on the earth with Jesus Christ. Isaiah 2:2-5 speaks of the bride of Christ and New Jerusalem when it says,

And it shall come to pass in the last days, that the mountain of the LORD'S house shall be established in the top of the mountains, and shall be exalted above the hills; and all nations shall flow unto it. And many people shall go and say, Come ye, and let us go up to the mountain of the LORD, to the house of the God of Jacob; and he will teach us of his ways, and we will walk in his paths: for out of Zion shall go forth the law, and the word of the LORD from Jerusalem. And he shall judge among the nations, and shall rebuke many people: and they shall beat their swords into plowshares, and their spears into pruning hooks: nation shall not lift up sword against nation, neither shall they learn war any more. O house of Jacob, come ye, and let us walk in the light of the LORD.

Revelation 21:24-25 continues this description,

And the nations of them which are saved shall walk in the light of it: and the kings of the earth do bring their glory and honor into it. And the gates of it shall not be shut at all by day: for there shall be no night there. And they shall bring the glory and honor of the nations into it. And there shall in no wise enter into it anything that defileth, neither whatsoever worketh abomination, or maketh a lie: but they which are written in the

Lamb's book of life.

Here we see a picture of the nations of the earth who failed to receive the Lord walking in the light of this holy city. Entrance into this city requires that your name be written in the Lamb's Book of Life. Those who commit abominations, tell lies, or are defiled are rejected from being a part of this heavenly city. When the kingdom of God comes to the earth, we see that New Jerusalem will be the center of the world that teaches the law of God and His judgments to those who have survived the tribulation. This idea of the great city of God judging those who reject Christ is not only referenced in these verses, but Christ Himself spoke this mystery to His disciples in Matthew 19. The account is given to us starting in verse 27.

Then answered Peter and said unto him, Behold, we have forsaken all, and followed thee; what shall we have therefore? And Jesus said unto them, Verily I say unto you, That ye which have followed me, in the regeneration when the Son of man shall sit in the throne of his glory, ye also shall sit upon twelve thrones, judging the twelve tribes of Israel. And every one that hath forsaken houses, or brethren, or sisters, or father, or mother, or wife, or children, or lands, for my name's sake, shall receive an hundredfold, and shall

inherit everlasting life.

There is a reward for those who make up the church of brotherly love. It is one of the greatest rewards you can imagine, an eternally close intimate relationship with Jesus Christ Himself. This church is not just a church of religious participation, but it is a group of people who are willing to give up everything to follow their one true love. This beautiful city has developed into the dwelling place of God Himself. It has become the place where Jesus Christ takes His abode and stays forever. Luke 22:28 give us a similar account. It says,

Ye are they which have continued with me in my temptations. And I appoint unto you a kingdom, as my Father hath appointed unto me; That ye may eat and drink at my table in my kingdom, and sit on thrones judging the twelve tribes of Israel.

The word Jesus uses for temptations is the Greek word *peirasmos* and means "the trial of man's fidelity, integrity, virtue, and constancy." The true bride of Christ has been proven through the trials of life and has remained faithful to Jesus Christ. This faithfulness rewards her as she takes her place to be married to her one true love. In the letter given to the church of Philadelphia, Jesus makes an astonishing statement He says in Revelation 3:8-9,

"for thou hast a little strength, and hast kept my word, and hast not denied my name. Behold, I will make them of the synagogue of Satan, which say they are Jews, and are not, but do lie; behold, I will make them to come and worship before thy feet, and to know that I have loved thee."

The Greek word for "worship" in this text gives us the picture of someone kissing a hand as a token of reverence. It also is defined as "reverence given to someone of superior rank." The bride of Christ will rule with Him and He will demand that respect is given to her. The bride is the home that Jesus Christ dwells in, and Jesus Christ is the center of her life. Without Him there is no authority, and without her He finds no dwelling place. Martin Luther may have given us an appropriate marriage analogy when he said, "Let the wife make the husband glad to come home, and let him make her sorry to see him leave."

As we continue to investigate this letter to

the church of Philadelphia we need to understand that this concept of Christ's inner dwelling and the bride's sincere love for her bridegroom is a relationship that has been tested and tried. It is not good enough just to profess a love for Jesus. Every believer will be proven with tests and trials. The core of every test sent our way tests our ability to obey the Lord, and our ability to sincerely love Him more than anything else. The amazing thing is that by obeying His Word we overcome every test and we find a new intimacy in our love walk with Him. Jesus continues His letter to His bride in Revelation 3:10. He says, ***"Because thou hast kept the word of my patience, I also will keep thee from the hour of temptation, which shall come upon all the world, to try them that dwell upon the earth."*** The bride's ability to faithfully endure and hold fast to the Word of God brings forth benefits for her that the other churches do not receive. This is revealed to us when Jesus says that this church has kept the Word of His patience. The word for "patience" in Greek is *hypomone* which means "one who tarries behind enduring and receiving ill treatment for keeping the faith." The picture presented to us is a bride that has endured great persecution and hardship, but still holds on to the Word of the One she loves. With every test and trial her obedience causes her to mature and grow into the true bride, ready to receive her Bridegroom. As the verse proceeds we see the time has come for the hour of judgment to fall upon the whole world, but she is kept from this hour because of the persecution she has already endured. So many people fail to see that God's coming judgment upon the earth is a righteous thing. It is the moment that the world reaps what it has sown. It is this judgment that brings about the fulfillment and the completion of the kingdom of God upon the earth. 2 Thessalonians 1:3-10 gives a complete account.

We are bound to thank God always for you, brethren, as it is meet, because that your faith groweth exceedingly, and the charity of every one of you all toward each other aboundeth; So that we ourselves glory in you in the churches of God for your patience and faith in all your persecutions and tribulations that ye endure: Which is a manifest token of the righteous judgment of God, that ye may be counted worthy of the kingdom of God, for which ye also suffer: Seeing it is a righteous thing with God to recompense tribulation to them that

trouble you; And to you who are troubled rest with us, when the Lord Jesus shall be revealed from heaven with his mighty angels, In flaming fire taking vengeance on them that know not God, and that obey not the gospel of our Lord Jesus Christ: Who shall be punished with everlasting destruction from the presence of the Lord, and from the glory of his power; When he shall come to be glorified in his saints, and to be admired in all them that believe (because our testimony among you was believed) in that day.

The bride of Christ is worthy of the kingdom because she has suffered with Christ and now she will reign with Jesus. Those who think that the last day judgment is unjust or unfair need to understand that nothing angers a man more than for someone to bring harm to his wife. Nothing will speed up God's impending judgment more than for the kingdoms of the earth to come up against the Church of the living God. For those who are in Jesus Christ; the kingdom of God being manifest upon the earth should be the greatest and most intense longing in our hearts. In fact Jesus said in Matthew 6:9-13 that we should pray for His kingdom to come and His will to be done in the earth as it is in heaven. The real reason men fear the kingdom of God is that deep down they know that the kingdoms of the earth will be turned to dust when the completion of the kingdom of God is manifest. Daniel 2:31-35 tells us what will happen to the kingdoms of the earth.

Thou, O king, sawest, and behold a great image. This great image, whose brightness was excellent, stood before thee; and the form thereof was terrible. This image's head was of fine gold, his breast and his arms of silver, his belly and his thighs of brass, His legs of iron, his feet part of iron and part of clay. Thou sawest till that a stone was cut out without hands, which smote the image upon his feet that were of iron and clay, and brake them to pieces. Then was the iron, the clay, the brass, the silver, and the gold, broken to pieces together, and became like the chaff of the summer threshing floors; and the wind carried them away, that no place was found for them: and the stone that smote the image became a great mountain, and filled the whole earth.

This vision was given to Nebuchadnezzar and Daniel interprets it. As the interpretation is given, it is revealed that the head of gold represents the kingdom of Nebuchadnezzar. Then the proceeding pieces of the image represent kingdoms to come. The stone that breaks all of the kingdoms and blows them away like the wind is the kingdom of God. This is revealed in verse 44.

And in the days of these kings shall the God of heaven set up a kingdom, which shall never be destroyed: and the kingdom shall not be left to other people, it shall break in pieces and consume all these kingdoms, and it shall stand for ever.

The coming kingdom of God will destroy all of the man-made kingdoms of the world and the earth's original intent will be re-established. In the last line of Nebuchadnezzar's vision we see that the stone becomes a great mountain that fills the whole earth. Earlier, we referenced Revelation Chapter 21 to establish the correlation between the church of Philadelphia, New Jerusalem, and the bride of Christ. I want us to return there and look at Revelation 21:10. It says, ***And he carried me away in the spirit to a great and high mountain, and shewed me that great city, the holy Jerusalem, descending out of heaven from God.*** Here we find John being taken to a high mountain to see the city of God or New Jerusalem coming down out of heaven. Some of you might think this is just coincidence, but Scripture tells us more about this mountain in Hebrews 12:18-29.

For ye are not come unto the mount that might be touched , and that burned with fire , nor unto blackness, gloom and darkness, and tempest , And the sound of a trumpet, and the voice of words; which voice they that heard entreated that the word should not be spoken to them any more: (For they could not endure that which was commanded, And if so much as a beast touch the mountain, it shall be stoned, or thrust through with a dart: And so terrible was the sight, that Moses said, I exceedingly fear and quake:) But ye are come unto mount Zion, and unto the city of the living God, the heavenly Jerusalem, and to an innumerable company of angels, To the general assembly and church of the firstborn, which are written in heaven, and to God the Judge of all, and to the spirits of just men made perfect, And to Jesus the mediator of the new covenant, and to the blood of sprinkling, that speaketh better things than that of Abel. See that ye refuse not him that speaketh. For if they escaped not who refused him that spake on earth, much more shall not we escape, if we turn away from him that speaketh from heaven: Whose voice then shook the earth: but now he hath promised, saying, Yet once more I shake not the earth only, but also heaven. And this word, Yet once more, signifieth the removing of those things that are shaken, as of things that are made, that those things which cannot be shaken may remain. Wherefore we receiving a kingdom which cannot be moved, let us have grace, whereby we may serve God acceptably with reverence and godly fear: For our God is

a consuming fire.

The mountain of God is Mount Zion God's holy city, New Jerusalem. We see angels, the general assembly of the Church of the firstborn, God the Judge of all, and the spirits of just men made perfect or mature, and the body of Jesus Himself. It is a kingdom that cannot be moved and those who enter there must have grace to serve God with reverence and respect. Isaiah 52 is another chapter that continues in the description of the mountain of God. You can find many prophetic references to Mount Zion, and the holy hill of God. This mountain is going to crush the kingdoms of this world and it will establish the kingdom of God forever.

Because the tribulation to come is righteous, there is no need for those who truly have a relationship with Jesus, to fear. The church of Philadelphia is told that they are kept from the hour of temptation that will come upon the whole world. Throughout history there has never been a time that the whole world went through a moment of God's judgment all at once, but you can be sure that, that day is coming. Many prophecy teachers reference Matthew Chapter 24 where Jesus talks about the great tribulation. This reference falls in line with Revelation and has to be taken very seriously. The hour of God's judgment will not be a pretty picture for the kingdoms of this world, or those who love the world and the things in it. For those of us who are in Jesus Christ, the coming days are not to be feared, but longed for. Many within the Church have a fear mentality concerning the coming of the kingdom of God. Those who fear need to re-evaluate their walk with the Lord. It is not God's judgment that brings about the kingdom; it is the maturity and perfecting of the bride that causes Jesus to come for his Church. When the bride becomes passionate about Jesus; we will see the fulfillment of the kingdom of God. There are too many congregations sitting in their churches expecting Jesus to come save them from impending doom. Yet they fail to realize that their personal disobedience to His Word and lack of fruit causes Him to tarry still. Jesus is not coming back for a bride that is weak and fearful. He makes His return for a mature bride measuring up to His stature. For years we have used the term rapture to speak of the day the bride is caught away, but the truth is that if the church you attend does not obey God's Word and bear forth the correct fruit the day of His return will be anything but rapture. Too many people want to be a part of God's Church for all the wrong reasons. They think if they walk the aisle and say a prayer that they will escape hell, and when it gets bad on the earth they think they can be raptured away. Only those who truly love the Lord and obey His Word will receive the benefits of being a part of His bride. The catching away of the bride will not occur until the bride is perfected and beautiful. Ephesians 5:25-27 says,

Husbands, love your wives, even as Christ also loved the church, and gave himself for it; That he might sanctify and cleanse it with the washing of water by the word, That he might present it to himself a glorious church, not having spot, or wrinkle, or any such thing; but that it should be holy and without blemish.

The Word of God is to wash us until we are able to be presentable to the Bridegroom. The bride is to be holy and this only comes through the great work of sanctification. Across our country, many denominations and organizations want to debate about the tribulation and what will happen to the Church. The only tribulation that the bride will go through is persecution from the kingdoms of the earth that is necessary for her perfection. Somehow earthly tribulation has always caused people to return to God. Once she is perfected she will be caught up from the earth. You may be saying how you can be so sure. Let's continue in our letter to the church of Philadelphia.

Behold, I come quickly: hold that fast which thou hast, that no man take thy crown. Him that overcometh will I make a pillar in the temple of my God, and he shall go no more out: and I will write upon him the name of my God, and the name of the city of my God, which is new Jerusalem, which cometh down out of heaven from my God: and I will write upon him my new name (Revelation 3:11-12).

The key to knowing we are going up is to also know that we are coming down. It is impossible for New Jerusalem to come down from heaven until first we are caught up to heaven. Again I will reference Revelation 21:2 it says,

And I John saw the holy city, new Jerusalem,

coming down from God out of heaven, prepared as a bride adorned for her husband.

Revelation 21:10 says,

And he carried me away in the spirit to a great and high mountain, and shewed me that great city, the holy Jerusalem, descending out of heaven from God.

These Scriptures verify that the bride will come down out of heaven. The word for "heaven" in Greek is *ouranos* and means "elevated to vaulted expanse of the sky where the seat of order of things eternal and consummately perfect dwells." This includes God and other heavenly beings. In the Greek the word for "heaven" and the word for "mountain" are connected. The word for "mountain" is *oros*. It means "a mountain lifting itself above the plain." At the root of the word for mountain is another Greek word called *airō*, it means, "to sail away to a place of happiness, power, and eternity." All of these meanings are in line with the description given to us in 1 Thessalonians 4:13-18.

But I would not have you to be ignorant, brethren, concerning them which are asleep, that ye sorrow not, even as others which have no hope. For if we believe that

Jesus died and rose again, even so them also which sleep in Jesus will God bring with him. For this we say unto you by the word of the Lord, that we which are alive and remain unto the coming of the Lord shall not prevent them which are asleep. For the Lord himself shall descend from heaven with a shout, with the voice of the archangel, and with the trump of God: and the dead in Christ shall rise first: Then we which are alive and remain shall be caught up together with them in the clouds, to meet the Lord in the air: and so shall we ever be with the Lord. Wherefore comfort one another with these words.

Here in Thessalonians we see those who are alive being caught up. The Greek word here is *harpazo* which means "to seize or carry off by force claiming for one's self eagerly." Jesus Christ is going to use force to take His bride. He is coming to claim her for Himself. In fact, He is eagerly awaiting the completion of her preparations so He can return. These are to be words of comfort and not words of fear. Revelation 22:13-17 says,

Blessed [are] they that do his commandments, that they may have right to the tree of life, and may enter in through the gates into the city. For without [are] dogs, and sorcerers, and whoremongers, and murderers, and idolaters, and whosoever loveth and maketh a lie. I Jesus have sent mine angel to testify unto you these

things in the churches. I am the root and the offspring of David, [and] the bright and morning star. And the Spirit and the bride say, Come. And let him that heareth say, Come. And let him that is athirst come. And whosoever will, let him take the water of life freely.

The true bride of Christ has a deep longing for her Lord and joins in unity with the Holy Spirit to say come. Too many congregations and denominations actually fear the coming of the Lord. The word "come" means in Greek, "to make one's appearance in order to establish." The real fear lies not in the coming of the kingdom, but in the lack of preparations being made by those who say they are waiting for Him. The true bride has great passion and will make preparations at any cost. These preparations are manifest in our lives through obedience to the Word of God by yielding to the work of the Holy Spirit. The church of brotherly love meets these requirements and anxiously awaits the return of the Lord.

At the very beginning of this chapter, I quoted 2 Peter 1:10-11 which gives each of us the command to make our calling and election sure. Those who will be a part of the church of Philadelphia will be those who go through the processes of God to ensure their entrance into the kingdom of God. Most of us have been taught that the sinner's prayer is the only process required making our election sure, but the fact is that if your conversion is real and authentic, the divine nature of Christ will be revealed in your life. This divine nature is the proof that your conversion is real and genuine. The texts in 2 Peter 1:2-11 will further define what I am trying to say.

Grace and peace be multiplied unto you through the knowledge of God, and of Jesus our Lord, According as his divine power hath given unto us all things that [pertain] unto life and godliness, through the knowledge of him that hath called us to glory and virtue: Whereby are given unto us exceeding great and precious promises: that by these ye might be partakers of the divine nature, having escaped the corruption that is in the world through lust. And beside this, giving all diligence, add to your faith virtue; and to virtue knowledge; And to knowledge temperance; and to temperance patience; and to patience godliness; And to godliness brotherly kindness; and to brotherly kindness charity. For if these things be in you, and abound, they make you that ye shall neither be barren nor unfruitful in the knowledge of our

Lord Jesus Christ. But he that lacketh these things is blind, and cannot see afar off, and hath forgotten that he was purged from his old sins. Wherefore the rather, brethren, give diligence to make your calling and election sure: for if ye do these things, ye shall never fall: For so an entrance shall be ministered unto you abundantly into the everlasting kingdom of our Lord and Savior Jesus Christ.

The only way to escape the judgment of the world is to refuse the corruption in the world. This comes by true conversion and by Jesus revealing His divine nature in your life. The true bride of Christ has diligently sought God by going through the processes of God to make her election sure so she will be allowed entrance into the kingdom of God. Peter takes us through these transformations that will lead us to the security of our election. Here is a summary of what is said here from the Greek. Be diligent to not only have faith, but press for serving God with excellence. By pressing for excellence you will attain knowledge of God, and when you know how God is you will gain self control, then self control leads to patience, patience leads to becoming like God, and Godliness makes you concerned for other Christians, until you finally have God's love. Faith is just the beginning of the process of becoming like Jesus. You notice how this progression leads us to the final stages of being able to love other Christians, then being able to love others like God loves. In this text, we find that both brotherly kindness and charity can be translated as "love." But when you look further you find that the Greek word for brotherly kindness is actually "Philadelphia" which is "love for your brother." The word "Philadelphia" is made from two Greek words. The second is *adelphos* which is "love for your own brother by blood." The first word is *philos* which has a very interesting definition associated with it. It is defined as "one of the bridegroom's friends who on his behalf asked the hand of the bride and rendered him various services in closing the marriage and celebrating the nuptials." This philadelphia kind of love not only reveals love for other Christians, but it reveals love for the bridegroom as well. The believer who takes the time to make sure others are married to Jesus demonstrates this love. The believer who is self-centered fails to go through these processes and will remain unfruitful and barren. In fact, this verse says that they will eventually fall because they are blind and have forgotten that Jesus set them free from sin to fulfill His purposes. The true bride has purposed in her heart that what is important to Jesus is important to her. She has decided to live with Him, and dwell with Him. She will not be complete until she is one with Him, and once this process is fulfilled she will love like Him. I pray each of us continue in obedience in our love walk with God so we will be allowed entrance into His everlasting kingdom becoming His bride and experiencing intimacy with our Lord forever.

Chapter 7

The People's Church

And he gave some, apostles; and some, prophets; and some, evangelists; and some, pastors and teachers; For the perfecting of the saints, for the work of the ministry, for the edifying of the body of Christ: Till we all come in the unity of the faith, and of the knowledge of the Son of God, unto a perfect man, unto the measure of the stature of the fulness of Christ: That we henceforth be no more children, tossed to and fro, and carried about with every wind of doctrine, by the sleight of men, and cunning craftiness, whereby they lie in wait to deceive; But speaking the truth in love, may grow up into him in all things, which is the head, even Christ: From whom the whole body fitly joined together and compacted by that which every joint supplieth, according to the effectual working in the measure of every part, maketh increase of the body unto the edifying of itself in love.

Ephesians 4:11-16

Over the last few chapters we have discovered that the concept of false religion is not limited to groups who follow other faiths, prophets, men, or deities. We have to accept the reality that there is false teaching and preaching among those who claim to be followers of Jesus Christ. If something is found to be false then it is not authentic. Jesus Himself wrote these letters to the churches. He addresses each church one by one and demands that they accept their faults and repent of their sins. In fact, by addressing the false doctrine He is giving each of us the opportunity to accept true doctrine in its place. Men do not make true doctrine. It is not something generated from a man's mind, or by a group of people making church policy. The Word of God should be the basis for everything we believe and practice within the Church. The true Church cannot be built on the concepts or ideas of men. In fact, those who are truly called of God will refuse to adapt God's Word to fulfill the desires of self. When self becomes involved in the building of churches, it causes the foundations of the Church to be weak and powerless. If the congregation is made to serve the agenda of the pastor the church is built on self. If the congregation is built to support and promote the ideas and doctrines of a denomination then this is self. When denominations and the "called of God" work overtime to please the people, bring in big numbers, and generate money, the motivating factor is self. The Church was not created to fulfill the will of man, but it is a body of people who have yielded their lives to fulfill the will of God. The time has come for self-will to yield to God's will. In all three of the previous accounts, the church is ruled by man to produce an outcome for self instead of the true intent of the Church being manifested. We discover a political system that yields itself to produce people who don't know God and pay money to have someone tell them that they do. The congregations determine what is preached and the denomination or so called man of God work overtime to keep the people happy to fulfill their personal lust for power and money. Across America, the majority of churches are organized and run on the basis of two prevailing political systems. The first type is an autocracy. Webster defines an "autocracy" as "a government in which one person has unlimited authority." Some congregations look to the pastor as the final authority, others look to the denomination as the final authority. In either case, men make the final decisions and determine what is best for the organization based on the pocketbook. The second type of governing organization is a democracy. Webster defines a "democracy" as "a government in which supreme power is vested in the people." The people use the vote to elect officials who give them what they want. The people hold all the power to determine what is right and wrong. Many denominations have integrated both systems into their government structures. The denomination rules from a distance holding the deed to the property, but allows the local body to vote to determine local government. If the denomination does not control the deed to the physical building, it still holds the ability to get rid of the man of God based on complaint. When it comes to the Church the primary form of government should be the theocracy. In this governing system, God is recognized as the supreme ruler. John 1:1-4 says,

In the beginning was the Word, and the Word was

with God, and the Word was God. The same was in the beginning with God. All things were made by him; and without him was not any thing made that was made. In him was life; and the life was the light of men.

This means that the Word of God is the final authority when it comes to establishment and governing of the Church. When we follow God's Word we will fulfill His will bringing the Church to His desired state of maturity.

Earlier in this book we addressed the church who believes that it is appropriate for the man of God to abuse the people in the church to fulfill personal lust. This is demonstrated to us in the chapter on the church of Pergamos. In reality, the congregation is partially responsible for the making of such men. Because the congregation has a desire to fulfill the lust of the flesh, it yields itself to men who let them see their desired result with their eyes. In reality, they have a longing to be like the man of God who drives a fancy car and yields himself to material gain. After a while jealousy sets in when they are not rich like he is and they begin to question this doctrine of wealth and prosperity, especially when the so-called man of God they created succumbs to some sort of hidden atrocious sin. Of course in this moment, the congregation or denomination is ready to call the man they created to accountability. They judge his moment of final failure with great recourse, but who judges the congregation or denomination for choosing a man that is led by the flesh in the first place. In the area of congregational democracy we assume that the congregation knows best. We allow the congregation and the denomination to determine what kind of minister they want, assuming they are already mature and able to make such decisions. How can a denomination out to build a worldly kingdom, or a group of congregational members led by the arm of the flesh decide who they want as their man of God? In this process of church democracy the only entity not voted on or selected through the democratic process is the congregational members themselves. The denomination really doesn't care what the people are like as long as the offering plates are full to the brim. The man of God has to serve the denomination, the board, and the people even if they are full of manipulation and self-serving agendas.

While there are many churches filled with man-made ministers, God is still appointing true men and women of God to fulfill His will today. In this world of denomination and congregational control, the true man of God finds himself in a precarious situation. Torn between the will of men and the will of God, he must choose which one he will serve and follow. Will he serve the people by making them think they are more than what they really are? If he fails to make the people happy, the denomination begins to threaten him by the revoke of ordination or license. True men and women of God must come to the realization that the denomination does not have the true power of ordination and license. God alone calls the true man of God, and his job is to make God happy above all else. It is the man of God's job to speak the Word of God whether it makes the people or the denomination happy or not. In John 10:25-30 Jesus tells us who the real people of God are.

" I told you, and ye believed not: the works that I do in my Father's name, they bear witness of me. But ye believe not, because ye are not of my sheep, as I said

unto you. My sheep hear my voice, and I know them, and they follow me: And I give unto them eternal life; and they shall never perish, neither shall any man pluck them out of my hand. My Father, which gave them me, is greater than all; and no man is able to pluck them out of my Father's hand. I and my Father are one.

The congregation that truly belongs to Jesus Christ wants to hear His voice above everything else. The true congregation of God believes the Word and will not let man pluck them out of God's hand. When the true Word of God is preached and you hate what you hear then God has a problem with you. The man of God should preach the whole Word and require that the congregation follow what it says. If denomination or the people decide what is believed and preached then there is no need for the Word of God at all. Let's look at John 8:47. ***He that is of God heareth God's words: ye therefore hear them not, because ye are not of God.*** Any part of the Word you reject makes a declaration to God that you are not His. There will come a day when God's vote comes in on the congregation that is really His. What we forget is that God casts the final ballot. His process is a one-vote system, and He is not into inclusion.

The idea that the congregation has the power to vote a man or woman of God into or out of position is not Biblical. Throughout the Bible we see God appoint men and women of God to lead His people. The people never voted on these individuals. The individuals were recognized as authentic through the truth they spoke and the signs that followed. The only passage of Scripture that even comes close to congregational choice, is given to us in Acts chapter 6 where the apostles asked the church to present seven men from among them to attend to church business. The apostles were the ones led by God and stated the requirements of God to the people.

Wherefore, brethren, look ye out among you seven men of honest report, full of the Holy Ghost and wisdom, whom we may appoint over this business. But we will give ourselves continually to prayer, and to the ministry of the word. And the saying pleased the whole multitude: and they chose Stephen, a man full of faith and of the Holy Ghost, and Philip, and Prochorus, and Nicanor, and Timon, and Parmenas, and Nicolas a proselyte of Antioch: Whom they set before the apostles: and when they

had prayed, they laid their hands on them. (Acts 6:3-6)

We see that God wanted men full of the Holy Ghost and wisdom, and also respected by the people. We also recognize that these choices were from among the congregation. These were not ministers coming in from the outside that no one in the local congregation knew. These men came from among them. The Word of God confirms this in I Thessalonians 5:12-13 where it says,

And we beseech you, brethren, to know them which labor among you, and are over you in the Lord, and admonish you; And to esteem them very highly in love for their work's sake. And be at peace among yourselves.

Even after the choices were presented, the apostles then had to approve them by the laying on of hands. If the people would have made a wrong choice I believe God would have revealed it to the men of God. While congregational members view the man of God as an elected official, Scripture gives us a completely different process. I will address the structure of true church government at another time, but every believer needs to be able to recognize the differences that exist between the true man of

God and a voted in official. One simple way of identifying the difference is that one plays politics like a true elected official, and the other speaks only the Word of God. Apostle Paul appointed men of God in all the churches he was affiliated with. In I Corinthians 7:17-24, we see direction given to them that are called.

But as God hath distributed to every man, as the Lord hath called everyone, so let him walk. And so ordain I in all churches. Is any man called being circumcised? let him not become uncircumcised. Is any called in uncircumcision? let him not be circumcised. Circumcision is nothing, and uncircumcision is nothing, but the keeping of the commandments of God. Let every man abide in the same calling wherein he was called. Art thou called being a servant? care not for it: but if thou mayest be made free, use it rather. For he that is called in the Lord, being a servant, is the Lord's freeman: likewise also he that is called, being free, is Christ's servant. Ye are bought with a price; be not ye the servants of men. Brethren, let every man, wherein he is called, therein abide with God.

Paul not only addresses the fact that God calls the individual, but then proceeds to address a religious question between the Jews and the Gentiles. The Jews believed that the man of God could only function in his office if he was circumcised, but Paul breaks religious separation by saying that God calls people circumcised and uncircumcised. Religion and denomination require things of men that go beyond what God requires. The religious systems of this world use doctrines to control men by seeking organizational approval. God is the only one who gives calling to men and He alone reveals what is required of them. The true man of God obeys the commandments of God, thus is his circumcision. If a man is called being a slave to the doctrines of men, he is now free to obey the Word of God alone. If he is called outside of a denominational faith or creed, he will now become a servant to the Word of God. Paul makes this statement clear reminding us that Jesus bought us. We owe our lives to Him. We will not be the servants of men. Elected officials owe their constituency. They have an obligation to serve the purposes of the people who elected them. They even have an obligation to their party. Denominationalism is no different. It requires the man of God to serve the people by holding forth the denominations doctrines. The man of God only serves the purposes of God. His job is to obey the Word of God.

The true man of God not only holds his life to account through obedience, but he also speaks out against sin and transgression that exist in the lives of God's people. God requires him to speak the truth of the Word of God without compromise. Those elected by the people will speak words that cause them to be re-elected over and over again. It does not matter if the messages preached send the individuals to hell; it's all about the people hearing what they want.

I charge thee therefore before God, and the Lord Jesus Christ, who shall judge the quick and the dead at his appearing and his kingdom; Preach the word; be instant in season, out of season; reprove, rebuke, exhort with all longsuffering and doctrine. For the time will come when they will not endure sound doctrine; but after their own lusts shall they heap to themselves teachers, having itching ears; And they shall turn away their ears from the truth, and shall be turned unto fables. But watch thou in all things, endure afflictions, do the work of an evangelist, make full proof of thy ministry. (2 Timothy 4:1-4)

The apostle Paul gives Timothy a direct

charge concerning his ability to prove that he is a real man of God. He reminds him that Jesus Christ is going to be judge. He then gives him a direct charge to preach the Word, no matter what season it is. God's Word never goes out of season and never changes with the times. It is all-powerful and will reprove, rebuke, and exhort the hearers. It teaches the man of God to suffer long with the people in the area of doctrine. It never turns the hearers to believe fables. In fact, this text talks about congregations and church members who will look to their favorite teachers for a good ear tickling. In the Greek the words for "heap unto themselves teachers" translates "individuals who accumulate in piles their favorite teachers." We are definitely in this time and season. Instead of the Bible being the primary book of the believer, the books of men have accumulated in the lives of those who say they are Christian. True servants of God follow the Word of God over every other book. In fact, they will teach the congregation to question the teachers by looking to the Bible for proof. The man of God has an obligation to preach all of the Word of God. The real reason the people do not want to hear the full Word of God is simply because it judges everyone of us and reveals areas of disbelief and sin. When the Word of God is preached, each of us has an obligation to believe it and follow it, even if we disagree with it. The more Scripture is given, the clearer the demands of God become. The Lord told Isaiah what he had to do.

Cry aloud, spare not, lift up thy voice like a trumpet, and show my people their transgression, and the house of Jacob their sins. Yet they seek me daily, and delight to know my ways, as a nation that did righteousness, and forsook not the ordinance of their God: they ask of me the ordinances of justice; they take delight in approaching to God. Wherefore have we fasted, say they, and thou seest not? wherefore have we afflicted our soul, and thou takest no knowledge? Behold, in the day of your fast ye find pleasure, and exact all your labors. Behold, ye fast for strife and debate, and to smite with the fist of wickedness: ye shall not fast as ye do this day, to make your voice to be heard on high (Isaiah 58:1-4).

As a man of God, Isaiah's job was to lift his voice like a trumpet. He was to cry aloud. By speaking God's Word, the peoples' sins and transgressions would be revealed. Israel didn't want to hear God's Word. They thought that the practice of religious ritual was enough. In appearance, it looked like they were seeking God's ways, but in actuality they were using religion to have a platform to bring up points of disagreement. The people thought that they could change the very Word of God through debate and strife. They thought that by obeying religious practices, it qualified them to lift their voices high and speak their mind concerning what God had spoken through the man of God. The people made the mistake of thinking that the man of God was the problem because he spoke the words, when in reality they had a problem with God. Too many congregational members think that attendance gives them the right to speak their minds. They want to have an opinion about what the preacher has said. True men of God will base all of their preaching on Scripture. They will rightly divide the Word of truth by backing up what is said, line upon line and precept upon precept. If the man of God is speaking God's Word and not his own, then judgment will surely come upon those who stand against him.

Not only do congregations and denominations have opinions, but many times their opinions are demonstrated through their faces. The man of God has to contend with the repercussions of speaking God's Word after he has spoken, but he also has to deal with the faces of men during the actual speaking. The ability to stand before the people and speak the truth of God no matter the outcome is a requirement for anyone who wants to be a true minister. The true man of God must speak God's Word without worrying about those he is speaking to. Ezekiel 3:4-9 says,

And he said unto me, Son of man, go, get thee unto the house of Israel, and speak with my words unto them. For thou art not sent to a people of a strange speech and of an hard language, but to the house of Israel; Not too many people of a strange speech and of an hard language, whose words thou canst not understand. Surely, had I sent thee to them, they would have hearkened unto thee. But the house of Israel will not hearken unto thee; for they will not hearken unto me: for all the house of Israel are impudent and hardhearted. Behold, I have made thy face strong against their faces, and thy forehead strong against their foreheads. As an adamant harder than flint have I made thy forehead: fear them not, neither be dismayed at their looks, though they

be a rebellious house.

Ezekiel was sent to speak to God's people. At first glance this sounds like an easy task. Our thinking says the people of God love God so they should love to hear Him speak. If only this type of idealistic thinking were true. God says it would have been easier if He would have sent Ezekiel to the heathen because they would have hearkened. Because of religion and denomination, the act of speaking God's Word to His people can be a very grueling and strenuous undertaking. This reality alone causes men of God to break down and yield to the people. But God tells Ezekiel not to look at their faces. God calls the people "impudent" and "hardhearted." In Hebrew, these words translate to mean "obstinate and stubborn." The definition for "obstinate" means "firmly or stubbornly adhering to one's purpose or opinion." All it takes to get God's people off course is to give them purpose or an opinion that goes against God's Word. Joining denomination and religion comes easy to God's people because they love to be difficult, they argue and fight. This fact alone is enough to drive the true men of God from the church.

It makes them pack their bags and head for the mission fields. It's time for the men of God to get backbones and be harder than the denominations and congregations that want to control them. We have to stand up and speak God's Word no matter who we offend. It doesn't matter if the congregation kicks you out and the denomination takes back its credentials. If God has called you then remain true to His Word and His judgment will bring the needed change. Man cannot take away from you what it had no authority to give. Jeremiah had a similar problem. He was sent to speak God's Word, except he was called to speak to the people in his early twenties. In Jeremiah Chapter 1, God tells him not to call himself a child. He tells him not to look at the people's faces, but to depend on God to deliver him. When God sent Jeremiah it was like God sending a young minister to speak His truth to the denominational leaders of his day. In Jeremiah 1:9-10 God reveals to Jeremiah what his obedience would do.

Then the LORD put forth his hand, and touched my mouth. And the LORD said unto me, Behold, I have put my words in thy mouth. See, I have this day set thee over the nations and over the kingdoms, to root out, and

to pull down, and to destroy, and to throw down, to build, and to plant.

In this Scripture we see the real reason that the people and the denominations have a problem with the obedient man of God. In the mouth of the man of God is the ability to uproot false teaching. When the Word of God is spoken, it pulls down and destroys false doctrines and man-made altars. In the Hebrew, we see a picture of the Word of God expelling or plucking up what has been established. God has given His Word to the man of God to release God's divine judgment on established religions or beliefs built by the hands of men. In fact, the Word of God is so powerful that it causes the false to vanish away. After it destroys the false, it rebuilds or re-establishes God's purposes in the hearts of men. It starts a new planting of God's Word in the lives of those who believe. It causes fruit to manifest to fulfill God's will. In this simple text we see how dangerous a true man of God really is. Through this man's obedience, what has taken denomination and congregation years to build can be torn down and vanish away by a single Word. Because of this fact, the man of God is silenced. He is taught to serve the agendas of men. Denomination and congregation control him. They train him to only focus on the building up and never on the tearing down. If the Word of God is never allowed to tear down man-made doctrine, then there is no true building or establishment within the Church. The Church is not the buildings and the assets controlled by the congregation or the denomination. The Church is the actual people sitting in the pews. When the man of God speaks the Words of God, it will cause those who are false to fall away from the Church. The true Word of God will not tickle the ears; it will speak forth God's will to the people. They then have a choice to follow or to disobey.

The majority of denominations or congregations believe that the loss of people is a sign that the devil is at work. If the true Word of God is preached and the congregation declines, this does not mean that the man of God is full of the devil. It might mean that the congregational members are. The truth is that without a following of people, man-made kingdoms cannot be maintained. The great thing about God is that His kingdom is going to come whether the people are for it or not. Another fact that needs to be considered is that God does not need our help to succeed. He is already a success, and men are the only ones in need. We are the ones who need His blessing in order to break the curse. The true man of God is not called to serve the agendas of men. He is called to serve the purposes of God. The true man of God not only follows through by being obedient, but he also develops the ability to repress his thoughts and believe God's Word. The true man of God is on a journey learning to speak only the mind of God. So many congregational members think that the ministry is an open door to state opinion, but the true man or woman of God has to speak the mind of God even when it goes against personal thinking or opinion. In Numbers Chapter 16, we see a group of men gathering themselves together to come against Moses and Aaron.

Now Korah, the son of Izhar, the son of Kohath, the son of Levi, and Dathan and Abiram, the sons of Eliab, and On, the son of Peleth, sons of Reuben, took men: And they rose up before Moses, with certain of the children

of Israel, two hundred and fifty princes of the assembly, famous in the congregation, men of renown: And they gathered themselves together against Moses and against Aaron, and said unto them, Ye take too much upon you, seeing all the congregation are holy, every one of them, and the LORD is among them: wherefore then lift ye up yourselves above the congregation of the LORD? (Numbers 16:1-3)

In these few lines of text we see Korah and a group of two-hundred and fifty princes rose up against Moses and Aaron questioning their leadership and authority. As the accusations come forth they accuse Moses and Aaron of doing too much. They also place the congregation on the same level as the men of God. They declare all of the murmuring Israelites as holy. This mindset is still manifested today in the form of congregational voting. Men of organizational power try to manipulate the man of God by telling him that the people have the final say. The Bible refers to these men as "men of renown." In Hebrew this means "men who had made a name for themselves on the earth." They are men who have the ability to bring forth great accomplishments in the natural. They are respected by men and therefore speak with a voice. In Scripture, the only other reference to these types of individuals is in Genesis 6:4-5. This text is linked to the merging of demonic angels with the daughters of men to bring forth giants in the earth. The Scripture refers to the seed of these sons of God as the men of renown. Whether the men of renown were the actual giants or the seed that followed this race, the merging of the demonic spirits with men brought forth tyrants in the earth. Men were so evil that God sent a flood upon the whole earth to destroy these types of individuals. Here in Numbers Chapter 16, we see this same spirit at work in these men who come up against Moses and Aaron. Among the assembly these men were princes, and rulers, who had a place of exalted position. Today, such men still rule and reign in the realms of religion and denomination. They question and correct the Word of God delivered by the man of God. They use religion and their social status to build earthly kingdoms to rule over. In the eyes of these men popularity is their key to control and power. Numbers 16:8-11 gives us an even further description of these men it says,

And Moses said unto Korah, Hear, I pray you, ye sons of Levi: Seemeth it but a small thing unto you, that the God of Israel hath separated you from the congregation of Israel, to bring you near to himself to do the service of the tabernacle of the LORD, and to stand before the congregation to minister unto them? And he hath brought thee near to him, and all thy brethren the sons of Levi with thee: and seek ye the priesthood also? For which cause both thou and all thy company are gathered together against the LORD: and what is Aaron, that ye murmur against him?

Not only were these men princes among the people, but also they were also born of the house of Levi, that allowed them to keep the house of God and minister to the congregation. Again, we see a picture of organized denominational leadership using the congregation to come against the men of God. While they had position within the house of God and could teach doctrine, they were not true men of God. Moses says that they desired the priesthood. In reality, they desired to control Aaron and Moses. In Numbers 16:28, the Word of God declares the difference that existed between Moses and these men.

And Moses said, Hereby ye shall know that the LORD hath sent me to do all these works; for I have not done

them of mine own mind. If these men die the common death of all men, or if they be visited after the visitation of all men; then the LORD hath not sent me. But if the LORD make a new thing, and the earth open her mouth, and swallow them up, with all that appertain unto them, and they go down quick into the pit; then ye shall understand that these men have provoked the LORD. And it came to pass, as he had made an end of speaking all these words, that the ground clave asunder that was under them: And the earth opened her mouth, and swallowed them up, and their houses, and all the men that appertained unto Korah, and all their goods. They, and all that appertained to them, went down alive into the pit, and the earth closed upon them: and they perished from among the congregation.

Moses did not devise a plan to make men follow him. In fact, he states that the works he had been sent to do were not generated from his own mind. The proof that Moses is not speaking of his own mind is always revealed after the Word of the Lord comes forth. In this instance, Moses says that if these men live to see natural deaths that they are of the Lord, but if the earth swallows them up he is hearing from God. Immediately, after he speaks the will of God, the men are destroyed and meet their doom. We are in a hour when God is calling true men and women of

God to speak the Word of God in the earth. We cannot cower to the religious organizations of men. We have to speak God's will and as we speak His mind He will demonstrate Himself in power and might. If we are going to speak God's will we cannot be controlled by congregation, denomination, or even self. We have to yield to God's purposes and plans. When it comes to God's will, we all need to understand that His will does not bend. We need to let the denominations and the congregations know that with God there is not a meeting of the minds. You will not sway God concerning His Word or His plans. God is not going to be called into a board meeting to give people an account for what He has done. He does not answer to us, we answer to Him. To be a part of Jesus Christ we must die to self and lay aside our worldly reputations to do His will. We have to lay our minds aside and take on one mind, and that is His.

Fulfil ye my joy, that ye be likeminded, having the same love, being of one accord, of one mind. Let nothing be done through strife or vain glory; but in lowliness of mind let each esteem other better than themselves. Look not every man on his own things, but every man also on

the things of others. Let this mind be in you, which was also in Christ Jesus: Who, being in the form of God, thought it not robbery to be equal with God: But made himself of no reputation, and took upon him the form of a servat, and was made in the likeness of men: And being found in fashion as a man, He humbled Himself, and became obedient unto death, even the death of the cross. (Phillipians 2:2-8)

God is calling the Church to a place of unity by getting rid of our personal thoughts and agendas. To be a servant of God, we have to be determined to have the mind of Jesus Christ.

The mind of Christ is not only demonstrated by speaking forth the Word of the Lord. It is also demonstrated by the man of God taking on the form of a servant. When we are obedient to adhere to the Word of God we serve the people we are trying to lead to God. Within our churches, there are multitudes of people who think they have been led to God, but actually they have been led to join a denomination or religious organization. When judgment comes, many will find that they were declared by men to be good Lutherans, or good

Baptists, or good Charismatics; but it won't matter what men have said when Jesus says, "I never knew you". The true man of God declares all of God's Word because He wants the people to escape judgment. He wants the people to obey the Lord on their own. Sometimes within the man of God there is great inward conflict. He has a true love for the people, yet at moments he has to speak forth truth that hurts. The true man of God only wants good for the people God has called him to, but when the people rise up against God's will, he must let God be judge. Many times people rise up with railing accusation and false statements against the man of God because their motivation to serve the Lord has simply been based on lust. In Numbers 16:12; we see Dathan and Abiram resisting Moses.

And Moses sent to call Dathan and Abiram, the sons of Eliab: which said, We will not come up: Is it a small thing that thou hast brought us up out of a land that floweth with milk and honey, to kill us in the wilderness, except thou make thyself altogether a prince over us? Moreover thou hast not brought us into a land that floweth with milk and honey, or given us inheritance of fields and vineyards: wilt thou put out the eyes of these men? we will not come up. And Moses was

very wroth, and said unto the LORD, Respect not thou their offering: I have not taken one ass from them, neither have I hurt one of them.

Not only did they resist his efforts to save them, they accused Moses of abusing his position of authority. Moses speaks to the Lord and asks Him not to respect their offering. He then responds to the accusation by saying that he has never taken a donkey from the people, or even hurt the people. True men of God don't manipulate to get, and they don't wish hurt to the people they serve. Because their heart is to lead God's people, they find themselves crying out to God in moments of God's judgment. Towards the end of Numbers chapter 16 the congregation blames Moses for the deaths of the men of renown.

But on the morrow all the congregation of the children of Israel murmured against Moses and against Aaron, saying, Ye have killed the people of the LORD. And it came to pass, when the congregation was gathered against Moses and against Aaron, that they looked toward the tabernacle of the congregation: and, behold, the cloud covered it, and the glory of the LORD appeared. And Moses and Aaron came before the tabernacle of the congregation. And the LORD spake unto Moses, saying,

Get you up from among this congregation, that I may consume them as in a moment. And they fell upon their faces. (Numbers 16:41-44)

True men and women of God fall on their faces and pray that God will spare the people in their congregations. After the congregation rose up against Aaron and Moses, these men of God fell on their faces and cried out to God. A plague went throughout the people. Moses tells Aaron to take incense and run between the porch and the altar to stop the plague, even after the crazy congregation has come against them. Moses and Aaron keep the hearts of true servants. Their willingness to help the people causes the plague to be stayed. Another example of this can be found in I Chronicles 21:16.

And David lifted up his eyes, and saw the angel of the LORD stand between the earth and the heaven, having a drawn sword in his hand stretched out over Jerusalem. Then David and the elders of Israel, who were clothed in sackcloth, fell upon their faces. And David said unto God, Is it not I that commanded the people to be numbered? even I it is that have sinned and done evil indeed; but as for these sheep, what have they done? let thine hand, I pray thee, O LORD my God, be on me, and on my father's house; but not on thy people, that they

should be plagued.

In this passage, David had made the mistake of numbering the people to determine his success. When he did, God's judgment was released on all of Jerusalem. David and the elders responded by falling on their faces in order to save the people. The fact is that mature men and women of God have a heart to save the people, not to harm them. Instead of using God's judgment as a form of retaliation, they use the truth of God's Word to bring the people to repentance. When people repent, the hand of God's judgment is stayed. When the man of God loves the people enough to speak God's Word and then pray for mercy concerning judgment, this is a sign of true maturity. In the reference in Chronicles, we see that David and the elders fell on their faces. The mature man of God seeks a balance between obedience to God and love for the people. This love for the people never changes the Word God asks him to speak, but it draws the man of God to a place of prayer and more submission for the sake of the people. The true elder will earnestly seek the Lord for the people that they might learn to give honor to God by placing Him in the utmost position of authority in their lives. We see a picture of this in Revelation 11:16 where it says,

And the four and twenty elders, which sat before God on their seats, fell upon their faces, and worshipped God, Saying, We give thee thanks, O Lord God Almighty, which art, and wast, and art to come; because thou hast taken to thee thy great power, and hast reigned.

The mature man or woman of God simply desires God to reign in the lives of the people. They recognize how powerful God is and have an earnest fear for those who would question His authority. Every denomination and congregation will give a personal account to God for not fearing Him enough to yield to the authority of His written Word. God is going to appoint true men and women of God to be a voice for Him in this hour. Once God uses them to speak His Word, judgment will come upon those who fail to receive it.

In Revelation 3:14-22, Jesus speaks to the church that has decided that the congregation is the final authority. He says,

"And unto the angel of the church of the Laodiceans write; These things saith the Amen, the faithful and true witness, the beginning of the creation of God; I know thy works, that thou art neither cold nor hot: I would thou wert cold or hot. So then because thou art lukewarm, and neither cold nor hot, I will spue thee out of my mouth. Because thou sayest, I am rich, and increased with goods, and have need of nothing; and knowest not that thou art wretched, and miserable, and poor, and blind, and naked: I counsel thee to buy of me gold tried in the fire, that thou mayest be rich; and white raiment, that thou mayest be clothed, and that the shame of thy nakedness do not appear; and anoint thine eyes with eye salve, that thou mayest see. As many as I love, I rebuke and chasten: be zealous therefore, and repent. Behold, I stand at the door, and knock: if any man hear my voice, and open the door, I will come in to him, and will sup with him, and he with me. To him that overcometh will I grant to sit with me in my throne, even as I also overcame, and am set down with my Father in his throne. He that hath an ear, let him hear what the Spirit saith unto the churches."

Every letter written to the various churches always starts by addressing the leadership of the church. What we need to understand is that first and foremost church leadership will be called to account for refusing to obey God's Word concerning church government, doctrine, and administration. The name of the church always has to do with the character or beliefs of the people who make up the congregation. In this case, the Greek meaning behind the name "Laodicea" can be summarized as "justice for the people." It can also mean "the people speak or give their opinion." The name "Laodicea" comes from two Greek words. The first is *Laos* which means "a great part of the population gathered together anywhere." *Laos* gives us a picture of groups of people gathered together to form a single governing body. The second Greek word is *Dika* which means "a judicial hearing, judicial decision, or a sentence of condemnation." When combined, these two words give us description of "a local body or believers who have set up court and decided by their own judgment what is right or wrong." In fact, condemnation seems to be the overall ruling when it comes time for judgment. According to Barna research and Ellison research, the average senior pastor presides over a church for five to seven years. When the statistic speaks of senior pastors; these are men who have been active in full-time ministry for around seventeen years and who are strong in their denomination affiliation. Most of the time these men have developed the skills needed to be at peace with the people, board, and denomination. These men have had multiple experiences in ministry and still find they have to leave the congregation God has called them to. Can you imagine how short their stay would be if they would require the congregation and board members to obey the Word of God? The Laodicean church has decided to let the people decide what is right and wrong. The people have been given the final say by vote and when they speak, someone will lose their job. Historically, Laodicea was one of the richest among the seven churches. This city was the banking center for all of Asia Minor. Around the time of 60 AD when Paul wrote a letter to the church, an earthquake devastated the city. When this happened, Rome extended a hand of support by offering assistance to Laodicia in the form of grants and tax relief. The Laodiceans refused Rome's help, and preferred to rebuild their city out of their own resources. Tacitus, a Roman Historian, wrote that the Laodicians decided to restore their city "with no help from us..." Apparently, this mindset was so strong among the people of the city that it spilled over into those who attended the church. The Laodician people were consumed with the idea that they decided their own destiny.

In Revelation 3:14 Jesus begins by letting the church know who He is and what He has the power to do. He says,

"These things saith the Amen, the faithful and true witness, the beginning of the creation of God; I know thy works, that thou art neither cold nor hot: I would thou wert cold or hot. So then because thou art lukewarm, and neither cold nor hot, I will spue thee out of my mouth."

Jesus says that He is the "Amen." In the Greek this simple word means, "so be it." It is a legal term that means, "this word stands." Jesus is the Word that will stand and judge. He is the only One with the true power to determine the destiny of the Church. As He continues, He describes Himself as the faithful and true witness. The Greek word for "witness" used here is one that implies "a legal witness or evidence in court." He then states that He is the beginning of the creation of God. When combined, the two Greek words for "beginning" and "creation" give us a statement. This statement declares, "Jesus is the principle rule and originator of institution and ordinance." In principle, the declaration He is making to the church of Laodicia is that He is the lawgiver and the judge. The Church is not built upon denomination, congregation, or minister; it is built upon Jesus alone. He alone determines those who belong to Him, and He alone has the power to judge the individuals He has called. The doctrine of judgment is His alone. He will not share it with congregation or denomination. Jesus is a just judge and judges those who are His by a completely different set of standards. He is not moved by numbers, success, or even by acquired possessions. He is moved by our ability to lay down personal opinion and be obedient.

He that rejecteth me, and receiveth not my words, hath one that judgeth him: the word that I have spoken, the same shall judge him in the last day. For I have not spoken of myself; but the Father which sent me, he gave me a commandment, what I should say, and what I should speak. And I know that his commandment is life

everlasting: whatsoever I speak therefore, even as the Father said unto me, so I speak. (John12:48-50)

The judgment that comes from Jesus is not based on the ability to have success with men; it is based on the acceptance or the rejection of the Word He has spoken. The very parts of the Word of God that we fail to accept will be the parts that judge us when we stand before Him. Failure to obey His Word causes us to fall short of His glory and His standard. As He proceeds in His indictment against Laodicia, He says that He knows their works are neither hot nor cold. The Greek word for "cold" is *psychos* which means "one who lacks mentally and is destitute of warm Christian faith and the desire for holiness." The word "hot" is *zestos* that means "fervour of mind to zeal or extreme action." The Laodicean church was not completely destitute of desire to follow Jesus, but they failed to have the zeal and passion required to sell out to the Word. They were lukewarm and Jesus the Word giver is going to regurgitate them out of His mouth. The mouth that vomits them out, is the mouth that speaks the Word of life. It is ironic that the same mouth used to give the Word, is the same mouth that is used to vomit out those who refuse to obey it. The Laodicean church has set itself up to be judged, and the Word they fail to receive is the Word that returns to haunt them.

Not only is there a return on the Word they have refused to obey, there is also a return on the words they have spoken. Jesus sees and knows all and begins to repeat the words this church had spoken about themselves. In Revelation 3:17 He says, ***"Because thou sayest, I am rich, and increased with goods, and have need of nothing."*** With the statement ***"Because thou sayest"***, He addresses this church's ability to use their mouth to speak their own words. Instead of making the Word of Jesus the primary authority, the Laodiceans love to hear themselves speak. They are so convincing that they deceive themselves into believing that they are more than what they are. James 1:22 speaks about this type of people when it says, ***"But be ye doers of the word, and not hearers only, deceiving your ownselves."*** In the Greek, we see a people who use their words to point out who they think they are. They are so busy keeping up appearances that they fail to realize that the knowledge they have attained does not give them authority to use it until they first live it. The members of the Laodicean church use religion as a means of control and status. They use their democracy to prove that they have the power to declare who a true man of God is. They proclaim out of their own mouth that they are rich. The word "rich" in Greek is *plousios* which means "abounding in material resources, rich in Christian virtues and eternal possessions." Their view of themselves is so high that they say they are "increased with goods." In Greek this means "they are able to pronounce salvation." They are so sure that they are saved and right that they have "need of nothing." Again the King James fails to adequately translate. The Greek word is *oudeis,* which actually means "no one or no man." The congregation of Laodicia actually has the mindset that it needs no minister or man of God. They think they are just fine and no one has the right to tell them their faults. Within themselves, they desire the power and authority to make the man of God subservient to their personal hogwash. They think they can make the man of God speak their words instead of God's. Jesus intentionally addresses their high-minded statements. He then starts the process of speaking the truth that devours them piece by piece.

In Revelation 3:17, Jesus gives an account of who these people really are. He says, ***"and knowest not that thou art wretched, and miserable, and poor, and blind, and naked."*** The first witness given out of His mouth is that they are wretched. The Greek word for "wretched" is formed from *talanton* that means "to weigh in the balance or scales" and *peira* which means "to make trial of a thing or a person." He uses this word to imply that the time has come for them to be laid in the balance in order to be tried. The evidence is going to be laid out before them and they will be brought to final judgment.

Surely men of low degree are vain, and men of high degree are a lie: to be laid in the balance, they are altogether lighter than vanity. Trust not in oppression, and become not vain in robbery: if riches increase, set not your heart upon them. God hath spoken once; twice have

I heard this; that power belongeth unto God. Also unto thee, O Lord, belongeth mercy: for thou renderest to every man according to his work. (Psalms 62:9-12)

God has all power and He is going to call every man to judgment. We cannot continue to deceive ourselves and think that judgment is only coming to the sinner. We have to understand that we will be judged based on obedience to His Word. We need to understand that all the riches in the world will not save us from the impending judgment of Jesus Christ. Making our natural efforts successful in the eyes of men will not cause the Lord's judgment to pass us by. Those who love Jesus have to come to the same realization as Paul where he says in Roman 7:21-24,

"I find then a law, that, when I would do good, evil is present with me. For I delight in the law of God after the inward man: But I see another law in my members, warring against the law of my mind, and bringing me into captivity to the law of sin which is in my members. O wretched man that I am! who shall deliver me from the body of this death?"

The power of the Word of God makes us all see that our flesh has a serious problem obeying what we know to be right. The Laodicean church has decided to silence the Word because it is too hard to hear that we are continually accountable to do what we know. Instead it's easier to try to become judge because then we are the ones who decide what is wrong in the lives of others. In this way we keep the focus off of ourselves. Jesus sees and knows all and is going to tell you who you really are. He says you're "miserable." This means "you are people without mercy who labor and toil to bring weariness." The Laodicean church spends its time toiling and working to fulfill the mischief it has in its heart. These people think that God has called them to work overtime to fulfill their divine calling of judging the man of God. Proverbs 24:1 gives us an accurate description, ***Be not thou envious against evil men, neither desire to be with them. For their heart studieth destruction, and their lips talk of mischief.*** These are like the men who came to speak wisdom to Job. They come with accusations against the man of God in order to explain something that is far beyond their human thinking. Job 16:1-5 says,

Then Job answered and said, I have heard many such things: miserable comforters are ye all. Shall vain

words have an end? or what emboldeneth thee that thou answerest? I also could speak as ye do: if your soul were in my soul's stead, I could heap up words against you, and shake mine head at you. But I would strengthen you with my mouth, and the moving of my lips should asswage your grief.

Instead of being a comfort to the man of God when the trial comes, they join the side of the enemy and continue to speak forth accusations. They become the voice of the enemy to bring the final blow of destruction to an already weary situation. Job says they are miserable comforters. They have come to gloat and boast during a time of the man of God's destruction. Jesus says that you are "poor." In Greek this means "you are destitute beggars." Jeremiah 5:1-4 speaks of spiritual poverty when it says,

Run ye to and fro through the streets of Jerusalem, and see now, and know, and seek in the broad places thereof, if ye can find a man, if there be any that executeth judgment, that seeketh the truth; and I will pardon it. And though they say, The LORD liveth; surely they swear falsely. O LORD, are not thine eyes upon the truth? thou hast stricken them, but they have not grieved; thou hast consumed them, but they have refused to receive correction: they have made their faces harder than a rock; they have refused to return. Therefore I said,

Surely these are poor; they are foolish: for they know not the way of the LORD, nor the judgment of their God.

If you can find a man that seeks to live the truth, you find a man that will be pardoned. Judgment was never meant for others, it was meant to be used to judge you. The Laodicean church declares that the Lord lives, but He is a God that lives only in their minds instead of in their actions. His judgment has stricken them, but they refuse to grieve. They refuse the correction He has sent to them. They are poor in truth, in judgment, and are destitute beggars. Begging God to save them, but failing in their knowledge of the truth concerning their own walk. Proverbs 13:7 give us wisdom that makes a declaration to those who will hear. ***There is that maketh himself rich, yet hath nothing: there is that maketh himself poor, yet hath great riches.*** If you are rich in self, you will never be rich towards God. If your feelings matter more than the condition of your spirit then you will remain poor in spiritual wisdom. Making yourself look good in the eyes of the congregation, denomination, or in your own eyes shows a lack of spiritual maturity. This same piece of wisdom is given to the man with great wealth in Luke 12:20-21, ***But God said unto him, Thou fool, this night thy soul shall be required of thee: then whose shall those things be, which thou hast provided? So is he that layeth up treasure for himself, and is not rich toward God.*** In the end, all of the selfish gain occurring within the church is going to be worthless because we fail to be rich in the things of God. The masses have become carnal beggars trying to get God to give them their selfish desires on the earth. Jesus speaks again to this carnal congregation and says, "You're blind." In Greek the word "blind" means "mentally blind, wrapped in smoke, conceited making foolish or stupid decisions." How can you judge anything when you are poor in the areas of truth and judgment in your own life? The denominational churches of our day continue to argue and bring up points of dissension. They fail to realize that the problem is not with the Word of God but their inward desire to control a people for gain. The Word of God is what it is and it says what it says. It has not changed. This same mentality has been birthed within the individuals in the congregation making them concerned with control instead of with their personal walk with the Lord. I Timothy 6:3-5 states,

These things teach and exhort. If any man teach otherwise, and consent not to wholesome words, even the words of our Lord Jesus Christ, and to the doctrine which is according to godliness; He is proud (blind), knowing nothing, but doting about questions and strives of words, whereof cometh envy, strife, railings, evil surmisings, perverse disputings of men of corrupt minds, and destitute of the truth, supposing that gain is godliness: from such withdraw thyself.

The proof that our teaching or doctrine is from God can be tested by the godliness of those we are teaching. Only the true doctrine of Jesus Christ will bring about godliness in the lives of the hearers. In fact, it will cause those who follow it to deal with self to the point of death. It requires us to obey the Word of God over the disputing of men. Here in Timothy, Paul gives a description of those who fail to follow Christ's teaching. They spend their time being blind. They constantly question and argue about the Word of God to the point of being consumed with their argument. While they are arguing they stimulate strife, and come up with evil thought up by the carnal understanding. When they speak, they assume and suppose that these thoughts are right. They continue in this process until they are perverted in their thinking and missing the point all together. They are destitute of the truth, the truth that Jesus Christ is the One changing the individual's life, not the denomination or the doctrine itself. In the end, these organizations think that gain is godliness. Paul tells Timothy to turn away from such individuals. We remain blind because we fail to crucify our selfish wants and motivations. The Word of God is at work judging us all. His truth is what we are called to adhere to. If we fail in our ability to back up our beliefs with the Word, then we judge others by the arm of the flesh. Those adhering to the doctrines of men as truth need to be careful in the area of judging other men; especially when we reject His truth and fail to grow in the things of God ourselves. Luke 6:37-46 gives us a great piece of wisdom.

Judge not, and ye shall not be judged: condemn not, and ye shall not be condemned: forgive, and ye shall be forgiven: Give, and it shall be given unto you; good measure, pressed down, and shaken together, and running over, shall men give into your bosom. For with

the same measure that ye mete withal it shall be measured to you again. And he spake a parable unto them, Can the blind lead the blind? shall they not both fall into the ditch? The disciple is not above his master: but every one that is perfect shall be as his master. And why beholdest thou the mote that is in thy brother's eye, but perceivest not the beam that is in thine own eye? Either how canst thou say to thy brother, Brother, let me pull out the mote that is in thine eye, when thou thyself beholdest not the beam that is in thine own eye? Thou hypocrite, cast out first the beam out of thine own eye, and then shalt thou see clearly to pull out the mote that is in thy brother's eye.

When it comes to asking men to live the Gospel, the measure we deal out to others comes directly back to us. If the Gospel is the final authority and we use it to bring others to salvation, those who are declared Christians will be brought to more account for their inability to follow its teachings. In this day and hour we have blind people who can't see their own problems telling other people what God has said. The true man of God is not afraid to admit his weaknesses and knows what God's Word requires of the people, will also be required of him. Jesus is dealing with us all, but our job is to deal with the beam in our own eye before we focus on our brother. It's hard to be a spiritual leader with your eyes shut.

The last indictment made against this congregation is in the area of nakedness. Jesus says, "You are naked." In Greek this means, "completely laid bare or exposed." This reference goes all the way back to the original sin of Adam and Eve. It takes us right back to Genesis 3:5-10, where the serpent deceived them.

For God doth know that in the day ye eat thereof, then your eyes shall be opened, and ye shall be as gods, knowing good and evil. And when the woman saw that the tree was good for food, and that it was pleasant to the eyes, and a tree to be desired to make one wise, she took of the fruit thereof, and did eat, and gave also unto her husband with her; and he did eat. And the eyes of them both were opened, and they knew that they were naked; and they sewed fig leaves together, and made themselves aprons. And they heard the voice of the LORD God walking in the garden in the cool of the day: and Adam and his wife hid themselves from the presence of the LORD God amongst the trees of the garden. And the LORD God called unto Adam, and said unto him, Where art thou? And he said, I heard thy voice in the garden,

and I was afraid, because I was naked; and I hid myself.

The Laodicean church is still trying to determine good and evil for itself. It continues to listen to the serpent's voice and chooses to believe his lies. If you want to play god in your own life and determine what is right and wrong for yourself, then be prepared to cover yourself when it comes time for judgment. To these individuals, hearing the truth of God's Word can be a scary thing, because deep down they know that they fail to follow it. For humanity, it is easier to believe a lie than to hear the truth. Practicing religion is the fig leaf response to knowing you're naked; obedience to Jesus is the acceptance of the final blood sacrifice given for sin in order to live the Word. The true reason the Laodicean church hates the truth of the Word is because it has the power to expose the nakedness. The idea of humanity being vulnerable means that there are consequences to the actions we choose. The Word of God exposes us and reveals the consequence giving us the opportunity to change as the truth is revealed.

For the word of God is quick, and powerful, and sharper than any two-edged sword, piercing even to the

dividing asunder of soul and spirit, and of the joints and marrow, and is a discerner of the thoughts and intents of the heart. Neither is there any creature that is not manifest in his sight: but all things are naked and opened unto the eyes of him with whom we have to do. (Hebrews 4:12-13)

The Laodicean church has been exposed and Jesus is the final authority when it comes to our salvation. He knows the mistakes we have made and longs to help us, but our response to the Word of God determines our inward thoughts and the intents of our hearts. If the Word of God is not preached, then the truth of the heart will not be revealed. If the church leadership only follows the Word part time, then our churches will be full of people whose intent is to only follow the Word sometimes. The Laodicean church wants be in control of their relationship with God. They want to determine what parts of God's instructions they will follow. They want to evaluate the Scripture and only do what is necessary. When you make Jesus Lord of your life, this is not how it works. Jesus is the One who tells the Church what to do. In Revelation 3:18 He says,

"I counsel thee to buy of me gold tried in the

fire, that thou mayest be rich; and white raiment, that thou mayest be clothed, and that the shame of thy nakedness do not appear; and anoint thine eyes with eye salve, that thou mayest see."

You cannot sit idly by and wait for everyone else to obey the Lord. You have to put your faith and trust in the Word of God and except all of its truth. Faith in the Word of God is what will bring you to the point of being gold. I Peter 1:6-9 says,

Wherein ye greatly rejoice, though now for a season, if need be, ye are in heaviness through manifold temptations: That the trial of your faith, being much more precious than of gold that perisheth, though it be tried with fire, might be found unto praise and honour and glory at the appearing of Jesus Christ: Whom having not seen, ye love; in whom, though now ye see him not, yet believing, ye rejoice with joy unspeakable and full of glory: Receiving the end of your faith, even the salvation of your souls.

Your faith will be tried and you will have to choose to believe the Word of God. Though you have not seen the Lord yet, by obeying His Word you already love Him. By believing His Word you are filled with joy and unspeakable glory. The final outcome is the receiving of your faith and salvation of your soul. If we fail to believe the Word of God, we lose something of extreme value. We lose our relationship with God. The Laodicean church wants to choose how involved they become with God, but all of us know that serving the Lord will cost you everything.

As Jesus reveals His Word of correction to the Laodiceans, the text builds to an ultimate climax in Revelation 3:19-20 where He makes a very weighty statement. He says,

"As many as I love, I rebuke and chasten: be zealous therefore, and repent. Behold, I stand at the door, and knock: if any man hear my voice, and open the door, I will come in to him, and will sup with him, and he with me."

The key to the restoration of the church of Laodicea is given in the form of chastening and rebuke. Because the church of Laodicea has made the choice to stop the man of God from speaking the Word of God, they have damaged their relationship with the God they say they love. Those with a sincere relationship with the Lord come to a place of maturity that causes them to have a longing for the truth.

Though the truth may be painful, the desire for a true relationship with Jesus outweighs the pain. Men have a natural fear of exposed sin, but first and foremost they should fear the Lord. When the Word of God is spoken, it is not the congregation's job to decide if they like it or not. It is our job to look to Scripture to seek the truth. True Christians have a desire to hear the un-compromised message of the Gospel. If the message is compromised then it loses its power, authority, and ability to set the hearer free. Those who want a watered down feel-good Gospel were never His to begin with.

Ye have not yet resisted unto blood, striving against sin. And ye have forgotten the exhortation which speaketh unto you as unto children, My son, despise not thou the chastening of the Lord, nor faint when thou art rebuked of him: For whom the Lord loveth he chasteneth, and scourgeth every son whom he receiveth. If ye endure chastening, God dealeth with you as with sons; for what son is he whom the father chasteneth not? But if ye be without chastisement, whereof all are partakers, then are ye bastards, and not sons. (Hebrews 12:4-8)

Most of us fail, simply because we refuse to try to do things God's way. Religion and denomination have made the Gospel a simple sinner's prayer instead of demanding the people to obey God to the point of blood. While many of us think we are full grown in the Lord we need to be reminded that true exhortation from God speaks to us as children. Those who desire to please the Lord must understand that He is the teacher and we are the students. True believers are ready to hear the Word of God and expect it to help them die to the flesh. Bastards are those who are born out of religion instead of the true bride. They are children that were not true sons, because the virgin they belonged to played the harlot. The Laodicean church that refuses to hear the true Word of God fails to be received because they fail to hear the truth. In Jeremiah 44, we find a similar attitude in the people of Isreal.

As for the word that thou hast spoken unto us in the name of the LORD, we will not hearken unto thee. But we will certainly do whatsoever thing goeth forth out of our own mouth, to burn incense unto the queen of heaven, and to pour out drink offerings unto her, as we have done, we, and our fathers, our kings, and our princes, in the cities of Judah, and in the streets of Jerusalem: for then had we plenty of victuals, and were well, and saw no evil. But since we left off to burn incense to the

queen of heaven, and to pour out drink offerings unto her, we have wanted all things, and have been consumed by the sword and by the famine. And when we burned incense to the queen of heaven, and poured out drink offerings unto her, did we make her cakes to worship her, and pour out drink offerings unto her, without our men? (Jeremiah 44:16-19)

Religious people are so arrogant that no matter how many men God sends to try to restore relationship, they still have the ability to reject the Word that has been spoken. If God cannot get through to this generation with the spoken Word it leaves Him no other choice except judgment. Judgment cannot be sent to a people until first they hear the Word. This is because once the Word is spoken they become accountable for hearing it. Religious people can be given the Word, but they fail to hear it because they believe what comes from their own mouths. Over my years in ministry, I have had the opportunity to talk to literally thousands of people across our great nation. As I recall many of the conversations, I am reminded of a common comment made to me by many who considered themselves to be strong believers. When asked about the Word of God that had been preached many gave this response. "Well, I know what you just said and what the Scripture said, but I believe ..." Outside of the Word of God it does not matter what any of us believe. Our churches are filled with people who think that what comes out of their mouths is the standard to live by. There are many people who take Scripture out of context and use it to justify the works of the flesh. A work of the flesh is something that fulfills or gives the flesh room to advance its earthly desire. The Word of God was given to kill the flesh, not to resurrect it. Religion lives by allowing the people to make the fleshly desires a spiritual work. You notice that the children of Israel were sacrificing to the queen of heaven so that they would have plenty of food and protection from evil on the earth. When Jeremiah gave them the Word of the Lord they refused it. So judgment comes from the Lord. While serving the Lord brings benefits in our natural lives, we need to understand that Jesus wants us to want Him more than even our own fleshly desires. To do this not only takes true love for the Lord, it also takes zeal to obey and zeal to repent. In the Greek the word for "zeal" means "to pursue that which is good, to have a strong desire or fervent spirit towards the things of God." Titus 2:11 tell us what it will take to see the Lord.

For the grace of God that bringeth salvation hath appeared to all men, teaching us that, denying ungodliness and worldly lusts, we should live soberly, righteously, and godly, in this present world; Looking for that blessed hope, and the glorious appearing of the great God and our Savior Jesus Christ; Who gave himself for us, that he might redeem us from all iniquity, and purify unto himself a peculiar people, zealous of good works. These things speak, and exhort, and rebuke with all authority. Let no man despise thee.

Paul tells Titus that He must speak things that line up with righteous and Godly living in the present world. At the end of this text he tells him to speak these things, exhort the people, and rebuke the people with all authority. Without the true Word of God being spoken by the man of God, the people will never develop true zeal to follow God. Without a desire to follow the Word of God, there will be no desire for true repentance.

To every true man and woman of God called by God to preach the Gospel, I want to speak directly to you and make you understand that God called you and He will hold you accountable for the way you deliver His Word. You are not called to make men happy; you are called to fulfill the desires of God. While doing His will takes courage and backbone, it is not your job to try to take vengeance on those who come against you. If you stand and obey God, He will handle all those that try to destroy you for speaking the truth. According to the 4th century Apostolic Constitutions, the first bishop of Laodicea was a man by the name of Archippus. Tradition states that he was one of the 72 disciples appointed by Jesus Christ in Luke 10:1. In Colossians we find a reference to Archippus in which Paul gives him specific instructions. Colossians 4:15-17 says,

Salute the brethren which are in Laodicea, and Nymphas, and the church which is in his house. And when this epistle is read among you, cause that it be read also in the church of the Laodiceans; and that ye likewise read the epistle from Laodicea. And say to Archippus, Take heed to the ministry which thou hast received in the

Lord, that thou fulfil it. The salutation by the hand of me Paul. Remember my bonds. Grace be with you. Amen.

Not only did Paul ask that the letter to the Colossians be read to the church of Laodicia, he also asks that the epistle he wrote to the Laodiceans be read to the Colossians. To date, the letter to the Laodiceans has never been found. Maybe this is because the Laodiceans got rid of the letter after they read what was in it. Of course this is mere speculation on my part, but if the people hated to hear from the man of God I am sure Paul was not well received. In this text Paul also tells Archippus to make sure he fulfills his ministry. In the Greek, the word for "ministry" means "those who by command are called by God to command and promote the Gospel." In essence, I believe that Paul was telling Archippus to not give in to the Laodiceans. He was calling him to account to be the bishop of the church and not let the membership run him. Another interesting thing about Archippus is the meaning of his name. In Greek his name means "to master the horse, to be chief, to lead, or to rule." In Scripture this is directly cross referenced to James 3.

Behold, we put bits in the horses' mouths, that they may obey us; and we turn about their whole body. Behold also the ships, which though they be so great, and are driven of fierce winds, yet are they turned about with a very small helm, whithersoever the governor listeth. Even so the tongue is a little member, and boasteth great things. Behold, how great a matter a little fire kindleth! And the tongue is a fire, a world of iniquity: so is the tongue among our members, that it defileth the whole body, and setteth on fire the course of nature; and it is set on fire of hell.

If Archippus is to master the opinions of the Laodiceans then he would first have to teach them to bridle their tongues. When the people run the church, it is easy for a man of God to lose his position simply by the people using their mouths to start fires that bring destruction. I believe David wrote about these types of people when he wrote Psalms 35:11-21,

False witnesses did rise up; they laid to my charge things that I knew not. They rewarded me evil for good to the spoiling of my soul. But as for me, when they were sick, my clothing was sackcloth: I humbled my soul with fasting; and my prayer returned into mine own bosom. I behaved myself as though he had been my friend or brother: I bowed down heavily, as one that mourneth for his mother. But in mine adversity they rejoiced, and gathered themselves together: yea, the abjects

gathered themselves together against me, and I knew it not; they did tear me, and ceased not: With hypocritical mockers in feasts, they gnashed upon me with their teeth. Lord, how long wilt thou look on? rescue my soul from their destructions, my darling from the lions. I will give thee thanks in the great congregation: I will praise thee among much people. Let not them that are mine enemies wrongfully rejoice over me: neither let them wink with the eye that hate me without a cause. For they speak not peace: but they devise deceitful matters against them that are quiet in the land. Yea, they opened their mouth wide against me, and said, Aha, aha, our eye hath seen it.

As a man of God, David knew the destructive nature of the people he tried to lead. Many times the man of God is accused of things he doesn't even know about. David says when the people rose against him; he continued to do what was right. He put on sackcloth when they were sick, fasted and prayed for the people, mourned for them as one would mourn for his own mother. But the people waited for adversity to come to David. They rejoiced when he was down. These types of people open their mouth against the true man of God saying what they think they have seen. In denomination and congregation alike there are multitudes of people waiting to destroy the true man of God, but if the true man of God will not yield and will only obey the Word of God to the point of passing the test, God's judgment will come to those who rise up. The church members that work overtime to destroy the men and women of God will come to judgment, if the man of God will not become wicked and give the correct responses. Paul tells Titus in Titus 2,

"But speak thou the things which become sound doctrine: That the aged men be sober, grave, temperate, sound in faith, in charity, in patience. The aged women likewise, that they be in behavior as becometh holiness, not false accusers, not given to much wine, teachers of good things; That they may teach the young women to be sober, to love their husbands, to love their children, To be discreet, chaste, keepers at home, good, obedient to their own husbands, that the Word of God be not blasphemed. Young men likewise exhort to be sober minded. In all things showing thyself a pattern of good works: in doctrine showing uncorruptness, gravity, sincerity, sound speech, that cannot be condemned; that he that is of the contrary part may be ashamed, having no evil thing to say of you."

As men and women of God we cannot determine what men will do to us, but we can be determined to do the right thing no matter what. To every board, denomination, church leader, and congregational member, James 3 continues to give a thorough description of the use of the tongue.

For every kind of beasts, and of birds, and of serpents, and of things in the sea, is tamed, and hath been tamed of mankind: But the tongue can no man tame; it is an unruly evil, full of deadly poison. Therewith bless we God, even the Father; and therewith curse we men, which are made after the similitude of God. Out of the same mouth proceedeth blessing and cursing. My brethren, these things ought not so to be. Doth a fountain send forth at the same place sweet water and bitter? Can the fig tree, my brethren, bear olive berries? either a vine, figs? so can no fountain both yield salt water and fresh. Who is a wise man and endued with knowledge among you? let him show out of a good conversation his works with meekness of wisdom. But if ye have bitter envying and strife in your hearts, glory not, and lie not against the truth. This wisdom descendeth not from above, but is earthly, sensual, and devilish. For where envying and strife is, there is confusion and every evil work. But the wisdom that is from above is first pure, then peaceable, gentle, and easy to be entreated, full of mercy and good fruits, without partiality, and without hypocrisy. And the fruit of righteousness is sown in peace of them that make peace. (James 3:7)

Know this that it is impossible for you to rightly judge when your tongue is used to bless men and curse men. The current church in our day has bitter and sweet water flowing from the same vessel. I agree with James when I say, these things should not be. Those who speak under the Spirit of true wisdom do so with a controlled tongue and meekness concerning this wisdom, knowing that they could possibly be wrong. If there is envy to prove your point, or strife in your hearts your wisdom is devilish. Demonic spirits are active and the result is confusion. True wisdom brings peace to the hearers. It contains the truth and the answer without showing partiality to one side or the other. It is simply the Word of God. To restore the Laodicean church to a state of commitment it is going to take men and women in leadership and in the congregation who desire to follow the Word of God without compromise. Instead of using the church to fulfill the lust of the flesh, we must be determined that God is the owner of his own people. He alone sets the standards and we learn to follow His truth.

Jesus is the Head

And He is the head of the body, the church: who is the beginning, the firstborn from the dead; that in all things he might have the preeminence. For it pleased the Father that in him should all fulness dwell; And, having made peace through the blood of His cross, by Him to reconcile all things unto Himself; by Him, I say, whether they be things in earth, or things in heaven. And you, that were sometime alienated and enemies in your mind by wicked works, yet now hath he reconciled In the body of his flesh through death, to present you holy and unblameable and unreproveable in his sight: If ye continue in the faith grounded and settled, and be not moved away from the hope of the gospel, which ye have heard, and which was preached to every creature which is under heaven; whereof I Paul am made a minister; Who now rejoice in my sufferings for you, and fill up that which is behind of the afflictions of Christ in my flesh for his body's sake, which is the church: Whereof I am made a minister, according to the dispensation of God which is given to me for you, to fulfil the word of God; Even the mystery which hath been hid from ages and from generations, but now is made manifest to his saints: To whom God would make known what is the riches of the

glory of this mystery among the Gentiles; which is Christ in you, the hope of glory: Whom we preach, warning every man, and teaching every man in all wisdom; that we may present every man perfect in Christ Jesus.

Colossians 1:18-28

Now that we have studied and considered the various belief systems of these individual churches, we must face the facts and realize that the day is coming when all man-made religion and faction is going to come to an end. God is not going to approve men for their works, but He is going to reprove men for not fulfilling His work. May the Lord open our eyes and make us see that the only work He has called us to be complete in, is the work of being obedient and yielded to His Word. It is so easy to get caught up in the success and accomplishment of man-made religion that we are blind to the fact we are failing to come to a place of completion ourselves. For our walk with God to be complete, we have to give Jesus the correct position in our lives. He will not be second to our denomination, congregation, or even to the beliefs we have set up in our own lives. To be complete, Jesus has to take His rightful position as Lord.

As ye have therefore received Christ Jesus the Lord, so walk ye in him: Rooted and built up in him, and stablished in the faith, as ye have been taught, abounding therein with thanksgiving. Beware lest any man spoil you through philosophy and vain deceit, after the tradition of men, after the rudiments of the world, and not after Christ. For in him dwelleth all the fulness of the Godhead bodily. And ye are complete in him, which is the head of all principality and power: In whom also ye are circumcised with the circumcision made without hands, in putting off the body of the sins of the flesh by the circumcision of Christ: Buried with him in baptism, wherein also ye are risen with him through the faith of the operation of God, who hath raised him from the dead. (Colossians 2:6-12)

The idea of giving Jesus Lordship in our lives has lost its popularity. The word "Lord" in the Greek is *kyrios.* It means "he to whom a person or thing belongs." It is a relationship between master and servant. It is learning to be so full of the Spirit of God that you seek to fulfill His will. Because Jesus was sacrifice for sin and God in the flesh, we need to understand that receiving Him is the first step in the process of making Him Lord. The verse we just referenced in Colossians tells us that holding to the rudiments or philosophies of this world will cause us to be spoiled or ruined. The word "spoiled" in Greek means "to affect what you will be." There is a state of completion in Jesus Christ that we are to walk in. If we fail to let Jesus be Lord of our lives through the work of His Spirit, then we will not be what we need to be. The word "complete" in Greek means "to be full or filled up, to be a vessel filled to perfection or completion." After we receive His atonement for sin, we need to realize that we are to be filled with Spirit of God to the point of complete fullness. The Word of God is the book that guides us to this place of complete or perfected obedience. The Holy Spirit is the One who teaches us to live the truth that is contained within its pages. The act of making Jesus Lord is more than just a single moment of confession. It is the process of learning to do what His Word asks of you. Matthew 7:21 tells us this when Jesus says, ***"Not every one that saith unto me, Lord, Lord, shall enter into the kingdom of heaven; but he that doeth the will of***

my Father which is in heaven." The Word of God is God's written will for those who will follow Him on planet earth. When it comes to belief we need to understand that we have to accept and apply all of the Word to be able to walk in the fullness of His will. I like to say that there are two things that will judge those who have a sincere desire to follow the Lord. These two items are time and teaching. The Holy Spirit will bring each of us the light of God's truth as we learn to continue to submit to Him over time and yield to Him as He teaches us. It is impossible to have true conversion and not be taught by the Holy Spirit. If Jesus is truly Lord of your life then you must learn to submit to His will and purpose. The process of maturity and growth requires us to submit to the knowledge of the Word each and every day. For many of us the problem is not in hearing the teaching, but it remains to be in the area of yielding to what we have been taught. We cannot say that Jesus is Lord and then continue to fulfill our lusts and desires over His wants and wishes.

In Malachi 1:6-8 God speaks directly to the leaders of the house of Israel, He says

"A son honoureth his father, and a servant his master: if then I be a father, where is mine honor? and if I be a master, where is my fear? saith the LORD of hosts unto you, O priests, that despise my name. And ye say, Wherein have we despised thy name? Ye offer polluted bread upon mine altar; and ye say, Wherein have we polluted thee? In that ye say, The table of the LORD is contemptible. And if ye offer the blind for sacrifice, is it not evil? and if ye offer the lame and sick, is it not evil? offer it now unto thy governor; will he be pleased with thee, or accept thy person?"

Honoring a man or a denomination does not qualify as giving honor to God. In religion we have been taught that the fulfillment of the religious obligation is the same as giving God a place of honor in our lives. The problem with this concept is that many of us are honoring men by obeying a tradition, but we fail to honor God because those who truly honor Him do things His way. Israel learned this lesson when God corrected them for giving Him offerings that did not meet the qualifications in His Word. Instead of following His instruction exactly they continued to adjust their practices to the minimum requirement. They decided what was good enough for God, based on what was comfortable for them. By doing things their way they were really fulfilling their own lust. God let's them know that He has the final say and He will reject things done the wrong way. He says that the offering was polluted and that He expected them to honor Him. In essence, the performance was a failure because acts of worship done our way will never be received. In Matthew 15:9 God says, ***"This people draweth nigh unto me with their mouth, and honoureth me with their lips; but their heart is far from me. But in vain they do worship me, teaching for doctrines the commandments of men."*** The heart of the issue is that those who really love the Lord will make every effort to obey the Scripture that is set before them. Those who are truly being led by the Spirit will obey the truth of God's Word above the doctrines, teachings, and traditions of men. In fact, when men add good ideas to God's Word, the believer will have to make a choice to follow the Word over the ideas of men that tend to make people more comfortable. Multitudes of people attend church Sunday after Sunday and think that they have fulfilled the performance God has demanded of them. They allow the denomination, the board, or the leader to make decisions of worship for them, instead of knowing what God requires for them. This creates worshippers who go through the motions, but have no heart-felt commitment to the truth of God. The text in Matthew 15 says that they worship God in vain. The word "vain" in Greek means "an effort that is fruitless because the individual has refused to consume, devour, and eat." Practicing Christianity out of a desire to please the pastor, organization, or denomination will never work. Until we learn to please God through obedience, the church will continue to produce half-hearted followers who fail to have true intimacy with the Lord. We can only grow and nourish ourselves by eating directly from the Word of God.

Colossians 2:16-23 says,

Let no man therefore judge you in meat, or in drink, or in respect of an holyday, or of the new moon, or of the Sabbath : Which are a shadow of things to come; but the body of Christ. Let no man beguile you of your

reward in a voluntary humility and worshipping of angels, intruding into those things which he hath not seen, vainly puffed up by his fleshly mind, And not holding the Head, from which all the body by joints and bands having nourishment ministered, and knit together, increaseth with the increase of God. Wherefore if ye be dead with Christ from the rudiments of the world, why, as though living in the world, are ye subject to ordinances, (Touch not; taste not; handle not; Which all are to perish with the using;) after the commandments and doctrines of men? Which things have indeed a show of wisdom in will worship, and humility, and neglecting of the body; not in any honour to the satisfying of the flesh.

Every believer needs to know that practicing religion is not the point of the Church. The point of the Church is to teach the individual to have intimacy with Jesus by learning to follow His Word through the act of personal obedience. Religion teaches the individual to follow the teachings of men. It lets other men determine when the individual has arrived. It also allows men to limit the individual's growth by determining how far he can go. The individual believer is restricted to only go as far as the religious organization has gone. Instead of teaching the individual to follow Jesus by learning to be obedient to the Holy Spirit and His Word, religion occupies the individual with the fulfillment of the traditions, or the moral do's and don'ts. Without the Word being the source, teaching the individual to have a personal relationship with Jesus, the individual is inundated with meat, drink, holy day, and religious practice. Paul tells the Colossians that these things will be dealt with in the future, but that the most important thing is that Jesus Christ takes His proper place. If Jesus Christ is given the correct place in your life all these things will follow. Paul warns the Colossians not to be taken advantage of men who would beguile them. The word "beguile" in Greek means, "to be deprived of one's reward or salvation." He then tells them not to be voluntarily humble when men tell them to worship angels. In Greek the description of the words for "worshipping angels" is "religious ritual or ceremony set up by a messenger." Religion teaches the followers to follow the teachings of men above the Word of God. This warning given by Paul says that those who continue in such teachings can actually lose their reward of salvation. The primary failure of these individuals is that they are not giving Jesus the head postion. Jesus Christ is to be given the primary position of authority in our lives when it comes to Christian relationship and service. Because Jesus is also known as the Word, obedience to Him is demonstrated by adhering to the rule of Scripture's authority by obeying it in the areas of church government, corporate worship, personal salvation, growth by dying to self, and increasing in the Spirit which leads to yielded obedience in our everyday lives. When we fail to give Jesus complete authority in our lives, we struggle to be set free from the nature of sin. Our flesh continues to live, and we continue to operate in disobedience. In fact, we keep the body of Christ from being nourished and increased with the increase of God. When Jesus increases in our lives we are set free from the actions of disobedience. We are taught to overcome sin by learning to yield to the Spirit of God and to His Word. Because the practice of religion fails to set the individual free, the individual is limited to the work of using personal will to try to stop the performance of sin. Here in Colossians 1:23 Paul calls this type of practice "will worship." It teaches the individual to overcome sin by self-control, but it fails because the flesh never dies.

The flesh continues to overrule those trying to do what is right. The only way to be totally set free from will worship is to have true intimate relationship with Jesus yourself. Every believer must love Him enough to obey His Word by learning to deny self and yield to the Spirit.

In the world of religion there seems to be a constant fight over what denomination or organization will prevail in its efforts to attain membership. Within every organization, men fight to come to power so that they will have their moment of divine rule or authority. Many congregations look to the pastor as the authority in the church, but this view is false. The leadership of the church is only in authority as they yield to the authority of Jesus Christ Himself, by obeying His Word. If the leadership fails to submit to the complete Word of God, their authority is diminished and they either learn to rely on religious works or personal gifts to make the people obey. For the Church to be complete, we must recognize that there is only One true head in the

Church and that head is Jesus Christ. If Jesus is the head and we are the body, we need to remember who the brain of the operation is. It is not our job to use our brains to make decisions about the Scripture we are called to preach. It is the job of Church leadership to preach the Word. Jesus is not a board member giving a suggestion, or a part time prophet who has shown up to show off His gift. He is God manifest in flesh. He has come to cause the natural body of man to be filled with the fullness of the Spirit, bringing us back to the state of Adam in the Garden. Instead of being led by the flesh, He has come to teach us how to reach a place of complete fullness in Him. Ephesians 1:19-23 tells us about Jesus when it says,

And what is the exceeding greatness of his power to us-ward who believe, according to the working of his mighty power, Which he wrought in Christ, when he raised him from the dead, and set him at his own right hand in the heavenly places, Far above all principality, and power, and might, and dominion, and every name that is named, not only in this world, but also in that which is to come: And hath put all things under his feet, and gave him to be the head over all things to the church, Which is his body, the fulness of him that filleth all in all.

This text reveals to us that Jesus was given all power and authority so that those who allow Him to be head of the body will be filled with the fullness of Him who fills all in all. Ephesians 1:18 says that this is the inheritance of the saints, that they would be filled with His mighty power. The body is the fullness of Him that fills all in all. In Greek we have the phrase *pleroma plural pas en pas.* This means "the body is the entity that has been filled with the complete richness or fullness of the presence of Jesus to the point that it completes His will by everyone individually and corporately coming to the complete state of being full." This same phrase is used again in Ephesians 4:11-16. It says,

(Now that he ascended, what is it but that he also descended first into the lower parts of the earth? He that descended is the same also that ascended up far above all heavens, that he might fill all things.) And he gave some, apostles; and some, prophets; and some, evangelists; and some, pastors and teachers; For the perfecting of the saints, for the work of the ministry, for the edifying of the body of Christ: Till we all come in the unity of the faith, and of the knowledge of the Son of God, unto a perfect man, unto the measure of the stature of the fulness of Christ: That we henceforth be no more

children, tossed to and fro, and carried about with every wind of doctrine, by the sleight of men, and cunning craftiness, whereby they lie in wait to deceive; But speaking the truth in love, may grow up into him in all things, which is the head, even Christ.

Jesus Christ ascended on high so that you and I would learn to be completely full of His divine nature and Spirit. Romans 8:29 speaks of this work when it tells us that ***"we are to conform to the image of the Son of God."*** The completion of this work happens as each of us yield to God by listening to the men of God who speak His mind as they are filled with the Spirit. By learning the truth of God's Word, obeying His Scripture, and yielding to His Spirit, unity will come to the point that the true Church will measure up to the complete work of Jesus Christ. This happens as Christ's doctrine replaces false doctrine and the Church is established in true teaching. The key that needs to be adhered to for these things to come to pass is allowing Jesus to fill all things. The Holy Spirit is the Spirit of Jesus and He was sent to indwell the believer. Within the world of the religious church there are many who claim salvation, but refuse to yield to the complete and full work of the Spirit. To call Jesus Lord, Jesus has to be given the head position so that He can fill every part of your life.

When Jesus purchased you, He bought you. The price He paid for your sin was the ultimate sacrifice that brings you back into communion with God's Spirit. He removed the sin from your life so that you might be filled with the Spirit of God as He was. The doctrine of Jesus Christ is that through the shed blood of Jesus Christ, man can be restored back to a state being full of the Spirit of God. Religion teaches us to practice morality by the arm of the flesh. It is impossible to give your life to Jesus Christ and remain in control. Either you will continue to control your life through your own thinking and your own works, or you will give yourself to God and obey His Word by yielding to the Spirit.

For they that are after the flesh do mind the things of the flesh; but they that are after the Spirit the things of the Spirit. For to be carnally minded is death; but to be spiritually minded is life and peace. Because the carnal mind is enmity against God: for it is not subject to the law of God, neither indeed can be. So then they that are in

the flesh cannot please God. But ye are not in the flesh, but in the Spirit, if so be that the Spirit of God dwell in you. Now if any man have not the Spirit of Christ, he is none of his. And if Christ be in you, the body is dead because of sin; but the Spirit is life because of righteousness. But if the Spirit of him that raised up Jesus from the dead dwell in you, he that raised up Christ from the dead shall also quicken your mortal bodies by his Spirit that dwelleth in you. Therefore, brethren, we are debtors, not to the flesh, to live after the flesh. For if ye live after the flesh, ye shall die: but if ye through the Spirit do mortify the deeds of the body, ye shall live. For as many as are led by the Spirit of God, they are the sons of God. (Romans 8:5-14)

The carnal Christian practicing religion continues to try to perform the Word of God through good works instead of dying to the flesh by being full of the Spirit. When religion and denomination teach its followers to follow man instead of God, the result is more works of the flesh. This text tells us that unless the Spirit of Christ dwells in you, you are none of His. It tells us that the Spirit will quicken our mortal bodies. It will cause the works of the flesh to die, teaching us to cut off the works of sin. Instead of continuing to be deceived by men who say that salvation is nothing more than a moment of confession, we need to understand that our confession of faith is in vain when we resist the Spirit of God who has come to take Lordship over our bodies. In church after church and denomination after denomination, men have been taught to profess Jesus as Lord with their mouths, but after profession they continue to resist the Spirit of Christ that comes to claim its Lordship. Members have been declared saved by church leaders who have taught them that the profession is more important than the Spirit. Religion says the work of confession outweighs the importance of the fullness of the Spirit. In fact, the majority of denominational believers have been taught to resist the Spirit of God. I have always wondered how people who proclaim themselves saved can be afraid of the Spirit of God, the seal of their salvation. So many people have been deceived. Every denomination and church that place limits on the work of the Spirit will be judged and declared to be false. 2 John 1:7-11 says,

For many deceivers are entered into the world, who confess not that Jesus Christ is come in the flesh. This is a deceiver and an antichrist. Look to yourselves, that we lose not those things which we have wrought, but that

we receive a full reward. Whosoever transgresseth, and abideth not in the doctrine of Christ, hath not God. He that abideth in the doctrine of Christ, he hath both the Father and the Son. If there come any unto you, and bring not this doctrine, receive him not into your house, neither bid him God speed: For he that biddeth him God speed is partaker of his evil deeds.

Here in 2 John we are told that deceivers have come into the world. A deceiver is recognized as one who cannot say that Jesus Christ "is" come in the flesh. Many denominations want to look at this text as a past tense statement. They want Jesus to come in the flesh to die for their sins, but they do not want Jesus to come into their flesh. Jesus Christ came to indwell the believer. This is the completion of the doctrine of Christ. When you accept Jesus and give Him Lordship through the work of the Spirit, He is come into your flesh and indwelled you to the point that changes have to happen. Those who preach a different doctrine than this, have not God. They are none of His. I Corinthians 3:16 gives this account. It says, ***Know ye not that ye are the temple of God, and that the Spirit of God dwelleth in you? If any man defile the temple of God, him shall God destroy; for the temple***

of God is holy, which ye are. True Christianity is practiced when the individual believer allows his temple to be indwelled by God. The fullness of the Spirit is the boldness that came upon the early Christians and caused them to preach even unto the point of death. The Holy Spirit is the present work of God that stands in the face of religion and says that God is demanding more.

Not only is God demanding more of the religious church, He is demanding more from the Church itself. As we continue to move closer and anticipate the coming of the Lord, we must continue in our pursuit for more of God. We have to give Jesus the ultimate place of authority in our lives by obeying His Word and yielding to His Spirit. We have to know the Lord by knowledge, obedience, and experience. Jesus is not something we practice; He is someone who lives in us. As true believers, we have to go past religion and denomination and become what He has called us to. We have to live to fulfill the will of God. We have to please the one who has called us. Paul tells

Timothy in 2 Timothy 1:8-14,

"Be not thou therefore ashamed of the testimony of our Lord, nor of me his prisoner: but be thou partaker of the afflictions of the gospel according to the power of God; Who hath saved us, and called us with an holy calling, not according to our works, but according to his own purpose and grace, which was given us in Christ Jesus before the world began, But is now made manifest by the appearing of our Savior Jesus Christ, who hath abolished death, and hath brought life and immortality to light through the gospel: Whereunto I am appointed a preacher, and an apostle, and a teacher of the Gentiles. For which cause I also suffer these things: nevertheless I am not ashamed: for I know whom I have believed, and am persuaded that he is able to keep that which I have committed unto him against that day. Hold fast the form of sound words, which thou hast heard of me, in faith and love which is in Christ Jesus. That good thing which was committed unto thee keep by the Holy Ghost which dwelleth in us."

It's time for the true Church to hold the doctrine of Jesus Christ without shame. We need to declare His power to the world, by practicing our faith no matter what comes. The reason Paul was able to suffer without watering down the Gospel is simply because Paul didn't practice religion, he knew God himself. He knew that God would fulfill His Word if he would continue in the true faith of Jesus Christ. He also knew that the only way to keep the true faith was through the work of the indwelling power of the Holy Ghost. If this was true for Paul, be sure that this same work will be required of those who call themselves the last day Church.

Reference List

Strong's Exhaustive Concordance of the Bible. James Strong. Nashville: Thomas Nelson Publishers, 1984.

Gesenius's Lexicon of the Old Testament. S.P. Tragelle. London: Samuel Bagster & Sons, 1857.

A Greek English Lexicon of the New Testament. Joseph Henry Thayer. 1889.

The Catholic Encyclopedia. Vol. 5. Simeon Vailhe. New York: Robert Appleton Company, 1909.

Seven Churches of Asia. In Wikipedia, The Free Encyclopedia. 2007-2009. http://en.wikipedia.org

Blue Letter Bible. 1996-2009. http://blueletterbible.org

For Booking, Products, or Ministry Training go to ferventfire.com.

To find us in Tulsa, OK.
Go to realchurchministries.com

To become a ministry partner write us at

Fervent Fire Ministries

315 S. Sheridan Road

Tulsa, OK 74112